UNSAFE SPACES

UNSAFE SPACES
Ending Sexual Abuse in Universities

By

Eva Tutchell
John Edmonds

United Kingdom – North America – Japan
India – Malaysia – China

Emerald Publishing Limited
Howard House, Wagon Lane, Bingley BD16 1WA, UK

First edition 2020

© 2020 Eva Tutchell and John Edmonds
Published under exclusive licence by Emerald Publishing Limited

Reprints and permissions service
Contact: permissions@emeraldinsight.com

No part of this book may be reproduced, stored in a retrieval system, transmitted in any form or by any means electronic, mechanical, photocopying, recording or otherwise without either the prior written permission of the publisher or a licence permitting restricted copying issued in the UK by The Copyright Licensing Agency and in the USA by The Copyright Clearance Center. Any opinions expressed in the chapters are those of the authors. Whilst Emerald makes every effort to ensure the quality and accuracy of its content, Emerald makes no representation implied or otherwise, as to the chapters' suitability and application and disclaims any warranties, express or implied, to their use.

British Library Cataloguing in Publication Data
A catalogue record for this book is available from the British Library

ISBN: 978-1-78973-062-3 (Print)
ISBN: 978-1-78973-059-3 (Online)
ISBN: 978-1-78973-061-6 (Epub)

INVESTOR IN PEOPLE

CONTENTS

BIOGRAPHIES OF EVA TUTCHELL AND JOHN EDMONDS	vii
AUTHORS' NOTE	ix
PREFACE	xi
1. A Scandal Concealed	1
2. Stories of Distress	31
3. Doubts and Discontent	63
4. Evidence from the Media	93
5. A Failing Process	107
6. Living with the Market	137
7. Seeking a Better Culture	161
8. Ending the Abuse	191
9. Regulation and Pressure	223
10. Starting Afresh	243
NOTES	247
GLOSSARY	259
INDEX	261

BIOGRAPHIES OF EVA TUTCHELL AND JOHN EDMONDS

Eva started out as a secondary school teacher and then worked for many years as an education adviser working with all age groups on gender issues.

Her book *Dolls and Dungarees* is recommended reading for primary school teachers. She has researched attitudes of teenage boys and published guidance for schools and colleges on disordered eating.

John was General Secretary of the GMB trade union for 17 years where he increased the representation of women throughout the union. He also served as TUC President. More recently John has focused on environmental issues, a more inclusive system of education and equal rights for women. He is a Visiting Fellow of King's College, London and a Visiting Professor at Durham University Business School.

Unsafe Spaces is the third book that Eva and John have written together. Their first, *Man Made: Why so few women are in positions of power*, is based on interviews with 115 successful women and was published in 2015. Their second, *The Stalled Revolution: is equality for women an impossible dream?*, studies the two most successful campaigns for women's rights in the twentieth century – Votes for Women and The Women's Liberation Movement – and suggests a pathway to a more equal and fulfilling society.

AUTHORS' NOTE

During the coronavirus lockdown the dearest wish of most of us was to get back to 'normal'. But as time passed, the mood has changed. Rather than looking backwards, we began to realise that we should try to create a way of life which is better than the one we left behind. In our research we discovered that, for many people at university, 'normal' means a life blighted by sexual harassment and abuse. The number of incidents is shamefully high and most universities are not coping well. Universities should forget about 'normal' and be more ambitious. They have an obligation to ensure a greater level of safety for their students and their staff.

PREFACE

We had no idea that sexual abuse was such a serious problem in higher education until, in the course of researching our previous book, *The Stalled Revolution*, we visited a London university. During our conversation with a member of the teaching staff, we were told that sexual harassment and abuse was very common on the campus – the word she used was 'rife'. When we expressed our shock, she suggested that we talk to a junior lecturer who had been assaulted by a senior colleague. Caroline (not her real name) was brave enough to tell us what happened to her, and her story is one of the many we tell in Chapter 2.

Once we began to research, it soon became apparent that sexual harassment and abuse in universities is far more prevalent and many of the incidents are much more serious than we had imagined. We decided that this largely unknown scandal needed to be exposed and solutions had to be found.

Our research has three main elements.

We **read everything** we could find on sexual abuse in universities. There was less than we expected although fortunately we were assisted by the valuable work of a few very distinguished scholars.

We made a **Freedom of Information (FOI) request** to all universities in England and Wales asking for the procedures which are used when complaints of sexual harassment and abuse are made. We also studied their policies. All 102 universities provided the information we asked for and we are very grateful for their cooperation.

The third element of our research is the most important. We conducted scores of **interviews** with people from all parts of the university community – students, academics, support staff, managers, administrators, Principals, Vice Chancellors and many victim/survivors. A number of organisations, including University and College Union (UCU), Universities UK (UUK), the Office for Students (OfS), the National Union of Students (NUS) and several Student Unions, were of great assistance.

We gave a **guarantee of confidentiality** to everyone we interviewed. We wanted to give victim/survivors a chance to speak without opening them to unwanted publicity and intrusive scrutiny. We also wanted to allow others, including very senior people, to speak freely without fear of adverse effects on their careers or their institutions.

Some interviewees have given us permission to use their names but, even in these circumstances, we have been cautious and only used a name when we are absolutely certain that the person concerned has taken full account of possible consequences. All the quotations are, of course, authentic and we identify what was said to us directly by using double inverted commas. We use single inverted commas for other quotations.

Early in our research we encountered a series of dilemmas about the language we should use. During the interviews we were told about a wide range of sexual misconduct. When we are sure of the nature of the abuse we use the specific term; we have avoided euphemisms as they can minimise the seriousness of the offence. Unfortunately, there is no word or phrase in common use to cover the whole spectrum of sexual misconduct including offensive language, sexual harassment, unwanted touching, stalking, unwanted sexual advances, sexual assault and rape. In this book we have used the term *sexual harassment and abuse* when we are referring to the complete range of sexually offensive behaviour.

Preface

We describe people who have endured sexual harassment and abuse as *victim/survivors*. This is a clumsy term but we regard it as appropriate. People brave enough to speak to us about their ordeal are undoubtedly survivors but they also deserve to be called victims to emphasise their suffering and to avoid the common implication that they are complicit in the offence.

For similar reasons we use the term *complainant* to describe a person who has submitted a report of a sexual harassment and abuse and the phrase *alleged perpetrator* to describe the person whom the complainant has accused. It was suggested to us that we might instead use 'reporter' and 'respondent'. We decide against these terms as they are imprecise and tend to diminish the seriousness of the alleged offence.

When writing about complainants and alleged perpetrators and in other circumstances where the sex of the person is unknown we have tried to be **gender neutral**. Although fair, the weakness of this approach is that it tends to obscure the fact that, in the vast majority of incidents, the victim is a woman and the perpetrator is a man. For reasons that we explain later, it is impossible to give precise numbers but, on the basis of the data which are available, it is likely that women are the victims in over 90% of cases. Our decision to be gender neutral also causes occasional clumsiness in the language.

Early in our research we decided not to indulge in a 'blame game'. We give the names of the relatively small number of universities who are doing well, but we decided **not to name (and shame) universities** which are doing badly. In fact there are a large number of universities whose performance is poor and naming a few of the worst would be invidious and might tend to encourage complacency in the rest.

In any event naming and shaming usually produces a defensive response and our motive in writing this book is not to get into a series of rows with universities but to press them to improve their performance. We write in the hope that, once universities better understand the gravity of the problem, they will address it more urgently and effectively than most have so far managed.

Many people helped us with information, ideas and opinions. We are particularly grateful to: Mags Alexander, Vicki Baar, Sally Barnes, Pauline Barrie, Anna Bull, Helen Carr, Rita Donaghy, Judy Dyson, Debbie Epstein, Michael Gold, Jayne Grant, Christina Green, Dan Guinness, Pierre and Etienne Hallien, Martha Jephcott, Susanna Jones, Linda Kirby, Sara Lasoye, Margaret Littlewood, Christine Megson, Amy Moran, Liz Nichols, Alison Phipps, Jack Rowland, Jan Royall, Amanda Sackur, Allan Savage, Heather Sevigny, Pam Taplow, Marinette Urvoy, Karli Wagener, Fiona Waye and Tom Wilson. Our Editor, Kim Chadwick, has given us great encouragement.

We agreed not to name our interviewees, but many of them will find their views and experiences described anonymously in the following chapters. Thanks to them all.

We also offer heartfelt thanks to the many victim/survivors who described their ordeal and its effects to us. For a number, this was the first time that they had told anyone.

We end with an offer. We have collected a great deal of detailed information about every university in England and Wales. If any university wishes to discuss these matters with us, we would be very happy to meet their representatives, in private if necessary. At the very least we could tell them about the practices and techniques which other universities have used, with some success, to reduce abuse and improve the culture of the campus.

1

A Scandal Concealed

The story of sexual abuse in universities is long and often unedifying.

Fifty years ago, many universities had their 'Dirty Dick' or 'Lester the Molester' who seemed to spend a good part of their time touching or propositioning women staff and students. Other men mostly grinned indulgently at these antics. Women who complained got little support. 'It is just the way he is', was the normal response, as if an inclination to prey on women is as excusable as short sight or deafness.

In Oxford University the behaviour of two predators has passed into legend. The Principal of Lady Margaret Hall is said to have stormed down to Corpus Christi College and demanded that Eduard Fraenkel, a celebrated classical scholar, be stopped from chasing after her women students.

Then there is the behaviour of the prominent historian Norman Stone. His obituary records that he did not visit Oxford often to do any teaching but

> '…on the occasions when he did appear… Stone became notorious for groping his female students …'[1]

Not just in Oxford, but in many universities sexual misconduct came to be regarded as so common and so amusing that it found a niche in fiction. In his introduction to a late edition of *Lucky Jim*, David Lodge remarks that a common theme of the so-called 'campus novels' was

> '...the taboo subject of sex between staff and students'.[2]

Whether taboo or not, readers seemed to appreciate the humour and few offered a word of censure. No wonder universities felt under no pressure to deal with the real-life miscreants in their midst.

Changes

Fortunately, in the 1970s the Women's Liberation Movement campaigned for a change in the way women were treated and Britain became rather less forgiving of sexual abuse. Universities changed too. Many more women were admitted as students, and some universities slowly began to look less like upper class boys' clubs and more like the community outside the campus.

Had this revolution been completed, perhaps universities would have developed the scholarly ethos of equality and mutual support which many hoped for. But universities have never entirely shed their gender bias. A sense of male entitlement still seems important in judgements about the value of research and in the appointment of senior academics.

If universities had changed more radically, perhaps sexual abuse would have withered away. But it never did. Instead, sexual misconduct in universities just faded from public view. It never seemed to appear on the political agenda. We asked a senior Minister who was in the Education Department during the early years of this century whether the issue of sexual abuse in universities had been brought to his attention. He told us that, as far as he could remember, it had never crossed his desk.

Even the scandals surrounding Savile, Weinstein and other notorious predators across society did not prompt much debate about what was going on in higher education. To awaken interest, the National Union of Students (NUS) conducted the first ever survey into sexual abuse in universities.

The results, published in 2010, were startling. A total 3,833 incidents were reported by 1,210 women. One in seven had suffered serious physical or sexual abuse; over two-thirds had suffered groping, flashing or unpleasant comments; a quarter had suffered unwanted sexual contact like kissing or touching; one in eight reported stalking. The NUS summed up the results by concluding

> '…higher education is not a safe place for women.'[3]

Surprisingly even this damning judgement did not produce much reaction in the media. Reports appeared in a few newspapers but there was little follow-up.

The change came in 2014 when *The Telegraph* commissioned its own survey and, in a series of powerful articles, demonstrated that sexual abuse was widespread in universities. Using the evidence from its survey, the newspaper approached Sajid Javid, then Business Secretary, and Jo Johnson, then Universities Minister, to demand that they deal with the problem. For more than six months nothing much happened, so *The Telegraph* threatened to run a campaign attacking the two ministers for ignoring a matter of great public importance. At that stage, Johnson wrote to Universities UK (UUK), the organisation representing universities, asking it, 'to take action to address the issues involved.'

The Telegraph regarded Johnson's initiative as feeble. It commented:

> "He's not publicly spoken about his commitment for change, and so far has achieved no concrete action."[4]

Nevertheless, feeble or not, UUK was rather affronted by Johnson's approach. Although a taskforce was set up apparently in response to Johnson's letter, UUK insisted that it was already tackling sexual abuse and that the taskforce was part of its ongoing programme.

Taskforce report

In 2016, the UUK Taskforce published its report:

> *Changing the culture: Report of the Universities UK Taskforce examining violence against women, harassment and hate crime affecting university students.*

The report concluded that the high incidence of sexual harassment and abuse in universities was 'unacceptable' and that universities should adopt a policy of zero tolerance. It drew attention to the 'positive action' which was being taken in a number of universities, but acknowledged that work to reduce sexual abuse was not 'systematic'.

The report made a range of recommendations,

> '…including (the greater involvement of) senior leadership, adopting an institution-wide approach, encouraging positive behaviours, working with the students' union and having effective governance, data collection and staff training.'

The Taskforce published 14 case studies and said it wanted to,

> '…facilitate the sharing of good practice across the university sector'

A Serious Problem

It was not difficult for the taskforce to reach the conclusion that universities had a serious problem and were not coping very well.

The Telegraph article which spurred the government into action had made very worrying claims. Nearly a third of female students, polled by the research organisation YouthSight, said they had been the victim of 'inappropriate touching or groping' and around 1 in 20 had experienced more intimate but unwelcome advances or been pressurised into sexual activity. Meanwhile one in eight male students had also been subjected to groping or unwanted advances.[5]

Public Health England commented on *The Telegraph* article by declaring that the situation was 'unacceptable.'[6]

Sarah Green, director of the End Violence against Women Coalition, was even more explicit.

> 'We currently have a situation where women in the workplace are accorded more protection than young women who live as well as study at university... This cannot be allowed to continue.'[7]

Meanwhile, a major scandal was developing in Sussex University, and it began to attract media attention at about the time the Taskforce was drafting its conclusions.

In December 2015 a senior lecturer at Sussex was charged with assault. He had beaten the postgraduate student with whom he was living and was convicted of the offence in the following June. The university did not suspend the senior lecturer until nine months after he was charged and only then after considerable criticism in the media.[8] When challenged, the university said, wrongly, that there was nothing the university could do until sentencing had taken place.

Many people in Sussex university were outraged by the university's apparent lack of concern. Faced with massive internal criticism, the incoming Vice Chancellor asked Professor Nicole Westmarland of Durham University to conduct a review. Her report was damning.

She exposed many examples of poor practice and said that the university had made its decisions on the basis of bad advice.

Media interest had now become intense. Newspapers were noisily researching the issue – inviting women who had been abused to contact their news desks. *The Independent* followed the Sussex case closely and was scathing in its criticism. *The Guardian* focused on the fact that the Sussex case concerned an assault by an academic on a student with whom he was sleeping. It found that abuse of this kind was common in universities. The first sentence of its article reads:

> 'The scale of sexual harassment and gender violence by UK university staff has been likened to the scandals involving the Catholic church and Jimmy Savile in accounts shared by more than 100 women with the Guardian.'[9]

Surveys

The years since 2016 have been filled with testimony from students and staff who have suffered sexual abuse. A number of important surveys have been conducted by the NUS, the Universities and College Union (UCU), national campaign groups and activists in particular universities. They all indicate that there is a major problem. Most show that the incidence of sexual abuse is high and is not diminishing.

In February 2018, the campaign group Revolt Sexual Assault, in partnership with The Student Room conducted a survey of 4,500 students and former students from 153 different institutions. It reported an appalling situation:

> 'Almost two thirds (62%) of students and graduates have experienced sexual violence at UK universities…

> This figure rises to 70% of female respondents, 48% of whom have experienced sexual assault, and 73% of respondents with a disability, where 54% have experienced sexual assault... A third of students (31%) felt pressured into doing something sexual.'

In 2019 the campaign group Brook commissioned an online survey conducted by Absolute Research. It was emailed out to thousands of students across the UK. A total of 5,649 replied and the results are based on their responses. The main conclusion is that

> '...more than half of UK university students across the country are being exposed to unwanted sexual behaviours such as inappropriate touching, explicit messages, cat-calling, being followed and/or being forced into sex or sexual acts.'[10]

The main form of abuse identified in the report is inappropriate touching. A total 49% of women said that they had suffered this abuse. The figure for men is 3%.

We also studied surveys conducted at particular universities. In one small university college over three quarters of women students replied to a Student Union questionnaire and just over half of them said they had experienced sexual assault. Another survey of a bigger cohort of students managed a response rate of close to 50%, and more than half of those replying said that they had suffered sexual harassment or assault. In 2017 *The Sun* newspaper carried out a survey in Durham University and, under the headline *Campus Sex Shame*, reported that:

> 'A shocking 48 per cent of female undergrads at Durham claim to have been attacked.'[11]

The NUS's 2010 report[12] had found that some students were being sexually abused by university staff. In 2017 the NUS conducted an online study in conjunction with the campaign group 1752[13] to explore this issue more fully.

A total of 1,839 current and former students took part. 4 out of 10 current students had experienced at least one instance of 'sexualised behaviour' from staff. Women were twice as likely as men to have suffered such sexual misconduct. Gay, queer and bisexual women were particularly likely to have been touched in a way which made them feel uncomfortable. Postgraduate students were more likely to suffer abuse than undergraduates.

Accuracy

There are differences between the results from these various surveys but they all reach the same conclusion: each survey shows that a very large number of students have suffered sexual abuse at universities. Sir Michael Barber, Chair of the Office for Students (OfS), described the survey results as, 'disturbing'.[14] This might be a careful understatement. Taken at face value, the survey results suggest that universities face a problem which is so serious that it could reasonably be described as an emergency.

The reaction of the universities to the survey results has varied significantly. Coventry University used the research carried out by the NUS[15] to reinforce its call for urgent action. On the other hand, the majority of universities made no public comment on any of the surveys. A few have cast doubt on the figures. One major university questioned the validity of the polling methods used in one of the national surveys and refused to circulate the questionnaire to its students.

The important question is whether these surveys give an accurate picture of sexual abuse in universities. One obvious concern can be dismissed very quickly. Surprise has been expressed in some universities that the number of students who say that they have been abused is so much higher than the number of complaints of sexual abuse actually recorded by the universities.

In fact the gap between the survey results and the number of reported complaints is easily explained. Only a very small proportion of people who suffer sexual abuse ever report it to the authorities. We examine the reasons in the next chapter, but the evidence of under-reporting is overwhelming. Some of the surveys we have quoted asked victim/survivors whether they had reported the abuse, and the number of students who said they had is very low.

> The first national survey, by the NUS in 2010, found that only one in five victims of sexual assault reported it to the university and a smaller proportion told the police.

> The survey commissioned by *The Telegraph* in 2014 found that almost half of the women who had suffered sexual assault or abuse at university, did not report their ordeal to anyone, even to friends or family. And six in 10 male victims also said they had told no one.

> The Revolt Survey in 2018 found even lower reporting figures. Only 6% of students who answered the survey said they had submitted a report to the university; 10% said they had reported it to the police.

> A year later the Brook survey added further detail. Even students who were forced into having sex were unlikely to make a report: only a quarter did so. Of the women who were inappropriately touched, only 5% reported it and, of the women who were sent unwanted sexually explicit messages, only 3% reported it.

Students who were sexually abused by staff are also very reluctant to report the incidents. According to the NUS/1752 study carried out in 2017, fewer than one in ten made a complaint to the university.

Critics of the survey results have also drawn attention to the fact that the proportion of students who say they have been abused, although always large, varies considerably between surveys. *The Telegraph* study suggests that about a third of students have suffered abuse, while others suggest about a half and the survey by Revolt suggests nearly two-thirds.

Part of the reason for these differences is that the surveys are collecting responses from different categories of students. Some surveys are confined to existing students, some include students from the recent past, some are limited to undergraduates and others include graduates studying for Masters' degrees or PhDs.

A second factor is that the definition of sexual abuse used in the surveys seems to vary. Some surveys focus on physical assaults, while others measure a wider range of misbehaviour. Obviously the narrower the definition, the lower will be the number of students affected.

A more substantial criticism concerns the survey methods. Very often the results have been presented by the media as if they are representative of the whole student community but this is rarely the case. Some of the surveys have collected their material by contacting a large number of students and asking them to report on their experiences. The survey results are based on the replies which are received. As some observers have pointed out, we cannot be sure that the students who reply are representative of all students. It is quite possible that students who have suffered sexual abuse are more likely to reply than those who have had no bad experiences. On the other hand, it could be that students with a miserable memory of sexual abuse are less likely to take part because completing a survey will mean recalling incidents which they want to forget. We have no way of knowing. So, if half of those replying say they have suffered sexual abuse, we cannot assume that means that half of the whole student population have been victims. It could be more or it could be less.

The NUS understands this issue very well and, in its report, *Power in the Academy*,[16] the NUS explicitly warns against using their material to calculate the prevalence of sexual abuse throughout the whole of the student community.

'This is not a prevalence study but a descriptive one.'

We attempted to discover which of the surveys were based on a self-selected group of respondents and which were based on the sort of polling which aims to produce genuinely representative results. It appears that the national survey conducted by Youthsight for *The Telegraph* and the Durham survey by *The Sun* were each based on the polling of a representative sample of students and the Absolute Research survey carried out for Brook might have been. The two local surveys we have quoted both had an extremely high participation rate and so would come close to providing a representation of the whole student community in those institutions. However, the Revolt figures, like the NUS results, were based on students who responded to their survey and do not claim to represent the student population as a whole.

So there is a mixture of methods and a range of figures. These surveys give a valuable insight into the extent of sexual abuse in universities but they do not allow us to say with absolute certainty how many students and members of staff are sexually abused each year.

In these circumstances, the best that can be done is to use the material which is available and the expertise of people working in this field to make an informed guestimate. Fortunately, when we pressed knowledgeable academics and university managers for their opinion on the prevalence of sexual harassment and abuse, we found some measure of agreement between them. Most suggested that probably about 15% of female students and perhaps 3% of male students are abused while they are at UK universities. On this basis it means that about 50,000 students are sexually abused each year.

Of course some of the ad hoc and local surveys suggest that the number of students who are abused might be much greater, perhaps as many as a third of women and 5% of men. On this basis the number of students suffering sexual abuse each year would be 100,000 or more.

These numbers are, by their nature, speculative and there are areas of particular uncertainty. Information about the sexual abuse of men is very unreliable. Men seem even more reluctant than women to report abuse and, as we found in our research, unwilling to come forward to discuss their experiences. The few gay men who have spoken suggest that the incidence might be well above the 3% figure which we have included in our calculation.

It should also be noted that our figures do not include members of staff. We can find no figures in the public domain which are sufficiently robust for us even to make a guestimate about the number of staff who are abused.

However, we can draw some conclusions. Even at 15% of women and 3% of men, the number of students sexually abused in UK universities is very high. Indeed, we think that the British public would be shocked by the suggestion that 50,000 or more university students are sexually abused each year. If that number were to become known and accepted, there is likely to be a major outcry and greatly increased demands for remedial action. This will be very uncomfortable for universities and perhaps for the Government, but it might lead to a change of attitude in higher education and make Vice Chancellors more determined to ensure that universities are safer places to work and study.

Sexual Abuse in all Its Forms

Universities know and share the reservations which we have expressed about the figures which are available. In the Introduction to the UUK's 2016 Report, *Changing the Culture*, the then Chief Executive of UUK, Nicola Dandridge, acknowledged that,

> 'On sexual violence explicitly, there is no comprehensive data available to indicate how many UK university students are affected by such incidents.'[17]

Nicola Dandridge is undoubtedly right, but the way she describes the dearth of information is a little worrying. We hope that her reference to sexual violence rather than to sexual harassment and abuse in all its forms does not reflect an unfortunate management view which was described to us by one highly placed academic who is deeply involved in her university's sexual abuse programme. She complained that it is only the serious sexual assaults which senior managers really care about. They seem to regard other forms of sexual abuse like the innuendoes, the offensive remarks, the explicit emails, the touching, patting and unwelcome sexual advances as too trivial to merit much attention. We disagree with that judgement.

In this book we take the view that every example of sexual abuse should be taken seriously and the culprits should be disciplined. We know from much research and from our many interviews that an environment where such behaviour is permitted creates anxiety and fear. It undermines self-confidence and pollutes the university environment.

We are reinforced in our view by the guidance given by the Advisory Conciliation and Arbitration Service (ACAS). ACAS has drafted the most authoritative definition of sexual harassment, a phrase it uses to describe all forms of sexual abuse. Although originally drafted to protect employees, the ACAS definition is widely accepted to cover other groups like students and volunteers.

ACAS starts by making it clear that,

> 'Sexual harassment is unwanted conduct of a sexual nature. It has the purpose or effect of violating the dignity of a worker, or creating an intimidating, hostile, degrading, humiliating or offensive environment for them.'

The guidance makes the crucial point that what matters is how the person, who is on the receiving end of the action, regards it. That well-used justification 'I did not mean it like that' is no defence.

> 'Something can still be considered sexual harassment even if the alleged harasser didn't mean for it to be. It also doesn't have to be intentionally directed at a specific person.'

Examples are given which make it clear that incidents which some people might consider as minor or even trivial are rightly regarded as sexual harassment:

- 'written or verbal comments of a sexual nature, such as remarks about an employee's appearance, questions about their sex life or offensive jokes;
- displaying pornographic or explicit images;
- emails with content of a sexual nature;
- unwanted physical contact and touching;
- sexual assault.'[18]

Everyone would accept that making suggestive remarks to someone who does not want to hear them is not as serious as carrying out a sexual assault. But that does not mean that the so-called 'lesser' offence should be tolerated. We record in Chapter 2 that a woman walking across the room in some university social gatherings can expect to hear remarks about her appearance and to have her bottom patted or smacked. There is no reason why women, or men for that matter, should be expected to put up with this behaviour. It should be called out as sexual harassment and the perpetrators should be required to stop. At a moment in history when the US President evidently thinks it is acceptable to grab a 'woman's pussy', it is important to emphasise that every form of sexual abuse should be condemned and eliminated.

The Information Gap

Unfortunately, the absence of what Nicola Dandridge calls 'comprehensive data' does not just apply to the sexual violence which she mentions. We do not have reliable information about:

- the prevalence of all forms of sexual harassment and abuse;
- the incidence of sexual harassment and abuse by gender;
- the extent to which lesbians and gays and people in transition suffer sexual harassment and abuse;
- the extent to which people with disabilities are affected;
- the extent to which people of different ages are affected;
- whether the problem is found to a similar extent throughout all universities or whether there are particular universities where students and staff are more at risk or where they are safer than average;
- whether students and staff in all academic disciplines are equally vulnerable;

- whether students and staff are equally vulnerable to sexual harassment and abuse at all stages in their university career;
- where and when sexual harassment and abuse is most likely to happen.

The information gap is enormous. In fact, senior management lack almost all the data which they need to understand the problem and to develop an effective programme to reduce, and ultimately eliminate, sexual harassment and abuse. In the present state of knowledge, university policy makers are trying to find a route through a difficult landscape without signposts and without a map.

In 2016 there was some hope this extraordinary deficiency would be corrected. Nicola Dandridge made it very clear that the UUK report, *Changing the Culture*,

> '...represents a starting point. More work is to come... I remain committed to progressing its excellent work. This will include building upon the case studies and the sharing of good practice identified in this report, so that across the sector and to the extent that it is possible, we can ensure that violence, harassment and hate crime affecting university students is a thing of the past.'

We asked UUK how this follow-up work is progressing. Professor Dame Janet Beer, who was then the President of UUK, decided not to meet us but referred us to UUK staff, who were helpful. We were told that the Taskforce was continuing its work and would produce further reports.

The first Review of progress since *Changing the Culture* was published in October 2019. We are grateful to the new President of UUK, Professor Julia Buckingham, for agreeing to discuss the Review with us. She highlighted some of the initiatives which have been taken and the determination of universities to make improvements. But she was frank in her overall assessment. As she recorded in her Foreword to the Review,

> 'There is however much more to be done, with progress still variable across the higher education sector.'[19]

Unfortunately, the Review makes no proposals about filling the information gap. When we pressed the issue, we were reminded that universities already hold a great deal of information about sexual abuse. That is true, but there are serious problems with the reliability of that material.

Every university keeps some sort of record of the number of complaints it receives, but these records do not reveal the extent of sexual abuse and give only an incomplete picture of its nature and distribution. We have already explained that most sexual abuse goes unreported; relying on the number of complaints gives a very incomplete picture. Moreover, while some universities record anonymous complaints, many others do not.

We also discovered that the manner of the record-keeping varies significantly. Some universities record complaints in great detail, while others focus on outcomes. To make matters worse, the way sexual abuse is categorised is not uniform.

The Australian Example

Australian universities have faced problems similar to those faced by British universities. There were many reports of sexual misconduct, and an increasing number of scandals were causing damaging publicity and political criticism. Universities Australia, which represents the 39 Australian universities, had made policy recommendations to its members but too little progress was being made.

The pressure to do more was considerable but Australian universities realised that, like Britain, they had too little reliable data about the extent and nature of their problem. So they decided that, if Australian universities were to develop credible and effective policies, this information gap had to be filled. After a good deal of hesitation and some political pressure, Universities Australia, agreed to ask the Australian Human Rights Commission to conduct a wide-ranging survey of university students.

The resulting report was published at the end of 2017. It is extensive. A total of 31,000 students took part and Universities Australia believe that the results give Australian universities,

> '…a greater insight into the nature, prevalence and reporting of sexual assault and harassment.'[20]

According to one senior manager, Universities Australia now has,

> '…a clear evidence base from which to make decisions and guide actions to prevent and address sexual assault and sexual harassment.'

The initiative seems to have been very successful both in providing the basis for future policy and in reassuring the Australian public and politicians that the universities are determined to tackle the problem. The survey has been both a practical and a public relations success.

British universities have been following events in Australia. *Changing the Culture* points to Australia (alongside the US) as a country 'seeking to address the same problems' as Britain and added,

> '…there is scope for the UK to learn from their experiences.'[21]

Reluctance

In our discussions we described the advantages secured by Universities Australia and the support which was developing in Britain for a similar survey.[22] We argued that universities need the data which would come from an authoritative survey, and without this essential information, policy initiatives will have to be based on guesswork.

At this stage our attention was drawn to the small budget of UUK. The Australian survey apparently cost the equivalent of £100,000. As there are over three times as many universities in the UK as in Australia, the cost of a similarly detailed survey in this country might cost about £350,000. After making further enquiries, we accept that UUK does not have the resources to pay for that sort of survey.

However, that should not be the end of the matter. Although UUK is relatively poor, even in its present straightened circumstances, the university sector as a whole is well able to fund a survey.

The annual income of universities in the UK is about £38billion. Paying for a survey on the Australian model would cost each university about £2,000 on average. Put another way, such a survey would cost about 25p per student. And of course this would be a one-off payment and is not a cost which would have to be borne every year.

We do not believe that any university could reasonably describe a one-off cost of £2,000 as unaffordable. Two of the Vice Chancellors whom we met made it clear that they were not against the idea of an Australian style survey. It was acknowledged that it would be helpful to have more detailed information, and one of the Vice Chancellors explicitly supported the concept of evidence-based decision-making. Nevertheless, commissioning a detailed survey does not seem to be very high on the priority list of most universities.

If the reluctance cannot be based on a shortage of funds, there must be some other explanation. Two possibilities have been suggested to us, and neither does any credit to the reputation of British universities.

The first is that the unwillingness to spend this relatively modest sum to collect essential information is an indication that the issue of sexual harassment and abuse is not, in reality, as important to universities as senior managers usually claim.

The second possibility is even more damaging. It was suggested to us that the reason for the present reluctance to collect detailed and accurate data may be because publication of the results of an authoritative survey would draw attention to a problem which universities would prefer to be kept well hidden. And, of course, it may well be that a survey would reveal that the situation is worse than senior managers have claimed.[23] Viewed in this way, a full-scale survey might seem a distinctly risky proposition.

Minimised

Whatever the correct explanation for the lack of enthusiasm shown by universities, a full-scale survey is certainly in the public interest. At present the myth persists that universities provide a safe environment for students and staff. The absence of reliable figures means that very few people appreciate how many university students and members of staff are sexually harassed and abused. Most parents do not consider the possibility that their daughters, and even their sons, might become the victims of sexual misconduct at university.

This lack of transparency is unreasonable. Potential students are entitled to know the level of risk they face from sexual harassment and abuse when they contemplate applying for a university place, and their parents certainly want to know. An authoritative survey would open the eyes of the general public to what is going on in higher education and warn them of the risk.

Stories of sexual abuse are regularly published but, until the last three years or so, journalists and politicians have been reluctant to dig below the surface. This was surprising in view of their deep interest in other university scandals. When it was discovered that the Vice Chancellor of the University of Bath was paid £468,000 a year, journalists and politicians were not prepared to accept bland assurances that the salary was exceptional. They wanted to examine the evidence to be sure that it did not indicate some country-wide inflation of Vice Chancellors' salaries.[24]

However, when the subject of interest was sexual abuse, the traditional approach has been much more forgiving. For many years, journalists and politicians have seemed content to regard each incident as a regrettable aberration instead of considering that it might be the symptom of a wider and systemic problem. Fortunately this rather smug attitude now seems to be changing. The tsunami of scandals which we describe in Chapter 4, with each month bringing a new story of misconduct and mismanagement, has punctured the complacency of earlier years and prompted more thorough investigations and more realistic conclusions. We trust that this trend will continue.

Keeping the true extent of sexual abuse away from journalists, politicians and the public is, of course, very convenient to universities. If the scale of the problem were to be recognised, the reputation of higher education would be damaged, the pressure for urgent and effective action would become irresistible, resources would have to be redirected and increased government regulation would become more likely. Until now, the universities have managed to avoid these unfortunate consequences by a mixture of good fortune and careful news management.

The good fortune arises in part from the rather casual way that the sex lives of students are regarded. Adults are inclined to think indulgently that universities are places where young people are permitted to discover and experiment with sex: a sort of *Love Island* on campus. When told of our research, one of our colleagues asked,

'Isn't it just kids mucking about?'

Stereotypes of student behaviour also get in the way of a proper understanding of what is going on: students are thought to drink a lot, take drugs and stay up half the night. With that mindset, no one is surprised if things go wrong from time to time: every fall from grace is regarded as regrettable but inevitable. When an 'unfortunate' incident occurs, there is a flurry of publicity, the university typically makes a statement about respect and 'zero tolerance', the public is reassured and the university is trusted to clear things up without the need for any outside interference.

The comforting story that each incident is exceptional continues to be the background message put out by universities every time sexual abuse is mentioned. When a university gets into the news because someone is known to have been sexually abused, the media will ask whether there have been other incidents. In most cases the university replies with complete accuracy that only a very small number of incidents have been reported.

Of course a fuller reply, which is rarely given, would point out that the under-reporting of sexual abuse incidents means that for every case reported there may be about ten other cases for which the university has no record. To qualify as a reported case, the complaint would normally have to be made formally and in writing; informal reports are often not listed. Although, and to their credit, a number of universities have begun to record complaints made anonymously, the majority still do not. The number of complaints recorded is further reduced because some complaints are withdrawn or closed down before the process of investigation and adjudication is completed. As one Student Union representative told us:

> 'If someone graduates before their complaint is dealt with, the complaint leaves with the student.'

By these various methods the problem of sexual abuse in universities is minimised. Available figures are quoted and no great dishonesty is involved. Yet, at every stage, a misleading impression is given and the public is encouraged to believe that there is nothing much to worry about.

Withdrawn

Nevertheless it is impossible to ignore some of the darker practices employed by some universities which have the effect of keeping the number of reported incidents as low as possible.

Many of the people we interviewed told us that their university, while apparently encouraging victims to report every incident, in practice did or said things which had the opposite effect.

> "I was warned that I would not want my complaint to define my time at uni."

At the moment when a victim makes a report of sexual harassment or abuse, their emotions are raw and the discussion has to be very carefully handled.

> "I had everything explained to me but it was done in a way that made me feel it would be best if I withdrew my complaint."

It is not clear whether this is ever the intention but, as we explain in Chapter 2, many of the victim/survivors we interviewed told us that the reaction of the person receiving the complaint is often downbeat and discouraging.

Whatever universities say in public, it has to be recognised that increasing the number of formal complaints increases the burden on university staff. Each complaint involves a great deal of extra work for Student Services and senior management. An investigating officer has to be appointed and no one is keen to undertake that task. The senior managers involved in any disciplinary hearing, and perhaps in an appeal, do not welcome the inevitable pressures. They know that the university might well suffer reputational damage if the incident is reported in the media. In addition, every university manager is aware that either or both of the persons involved, complainant and accused, might take legal action against the university or against each other. We do not have to question the good faith of the staff and managers involved in processing a complaint to recognise that there might be a sense of relief when a complaint is withdrawn.

Secrecy

All universities promise to keep the process of reporting and investigating a complaint of sexual abuse as confidential as possible. This reassures the person submitting the complaint and seems to be even-handed in preventing both the complainant and the university from speaking about the case. However, it does not always seem very fair to the victim/survivor. While the complainant is required to say nothing to anyone, the university retains the right to make general statements about its policy, providing it does not mention the particular case. This often makes the victim/survivor feel isolated and vulnerable. One woman in this position told us,

> "At first I thought that the confidentiality was there to protect me but I then realised that it was more important to the university. It shut me up while the university seemed to say anything it wanted."

A senior academic in another university is sure that the commitment to confidentiality is regularly used to protect the reputation of the university.

> "In the system there is an obsession with secrecy. At first I thought that it was there to protect the victim but then I realised that procedures which are conducted in secret mean that there is no scrutiny."

On occasion, universities have sought to keep matters secret by behaviour which, when it became public, has opened them to considerable criticism. Several universities have apparently pressed victim/survivors into signing non-disclosure agreements (NDAs) to prevent them talking about the sexual abuse which they suffered. NDAs were originally designed to stop staff passing on trade secrets if they changed jobs. There seemed to be a general agreement they are not appropriate in abuse cases. When one university was alleged to have paid nearly £400,000 in NDAs over a five-year period to prevent a number of complainants speaking out about their sexual abuse, it was still assumed that this was exceptional and the practice was quickly condemned.

The comfortable assumption that NDAs were rarely used began to unravel as the experience suffered by the astrophysicist Emma Chapman became widely known. She took a complaint of harassment against a staff member at University College, London. She expected the case to be settled in six weeks but it lasted nearly two years. She was pressed to sign a NDA and was only able to speak out after she won what she termed

> '…a precedent-setting confidentiality waiver that enabled me to break the silence on everything that happened to me and on how institutional policy enabled a horrific experience.'[25]

What was a worrying possibility soon became an established fact. It had now become clear that the use of NDAs in abuse cases was not exceptional; it had become routine. In 2019 the BBC published evidence which showed that 96 universities in the UK had spent £87m on around 4,000 settlements in the two years or so since 2017. The number of universities and the number of NDA settlements was far greater than most people had imagined. Some of the ancillary information was also extraordinary. Apparently not all universities record the issue when they pay out the money. So it is not clear exactly how many of these NDAs relate to bullying, harassment and sexual misconduct. But it is not disputed by the universities that a sizable proportion of the cases involve sexual abuse.[26] The BBC's revelation brought heavy criticism of the practice by Chris Skidmore, then Government Minister for Universities. He said

> 'Let me be clear that any use of this sort of agreement to silence people or hide details of unfair practices is an outrage and risks bringing the reputation of our world-leading higher education system into disrepute.'[27]

There was also a statement from UUK saying that NDAs should not be used to keep victims quiet in abuse and bullying cases. Time will tell whether universities take this advice.

Reputation

The Minister's strictures are deserved. The use of NDAs is incompatible with the claim of universities to be liberal and moral organisations. But we hope that the Minister and his successors will reflect on why universities decided to use NDAs in the first place. Universities were tempted to use these squalid instruments to protect the institution from the reputational damage which would occur if the public were to realise the full extent of sexual abuse in universities. In Chapter 6 we explain how, in the very competitive market which the Government has created, damage to reputation can soon lead to a rapid drop in applications from potential students and to financial difficulties for the university. It is inappropriate to exhort universities to take a high moral position unless it is recognised that creating a commercial and competitive structure for higher education is liable to encourage the kind of short-term fixes which are relatively common in the corporate world.

The disgraceful incidents which occurred at Warwick University in 2018 and 2019 demonstrate the lengths to which some universities are prepared to go as they strive to restrict reputational damage. The full story of the Warwick scandal is told in the next chapter. Here we only consider the actions of the university's management when it first received a complaint that a group of male students had established a network exchanging vile messages which contemplated the rape and sexual assault of female students.

Very quickly the University appointed an investigator to establish the facts. It might be expected that the investigator would be fully trained to understand the nature of sexual misconduct and how it affects its victims. This was particularly important because the emails written by the men in the network were actually naming women whom, they said, 'deserved' to be raped. And one of the women named was the complainant.

On a Friday evening at 10p.m. the investigator wrote to one of the women and asked to see her early on the following Tuesday. That was when the investigator's identity was revealed. Amazingly, the person appointed to be the investigator was Peter Dunn, the Director of Press and Media Relations for Warwick University. Since he was the representative of the university who would answer questions from the media about the rape emails, he was asked how he could avoid the obvious conflict of interest. He said he would delegate his press role to someone else. There is no evidence that he ever did so.

It got worse. When Dunn met the complainant, she was horrified by his line of questioning. He asked her whether she had a sexual relationship with any of the men involved; he asked her about each one in turn. She said that she felt that she, and not the men, was on trial. Dunn continued to make statements which seemed to be intended to discredit the women. In his report, he said that there are 'discrepancies' in the women's stories and that one of the women was not a reliable witness.

Eleven men were questioned by Dunn and the questioning revealed that although their original chat line had been shut down, they had started a new chat line and had showed no sign of remorse. Dunn's verdict was that two men were innocent, three were guilty of minor offences and six were guilty of major offences. The women whom Dunn interviewed were particularly upset at the suggestion that some of the men had only committed a 'minor' offence. One woman pointed out that the example of a minor offence which was usually quoted was bringing an ASDA trolley onto campus.

No one has explained why Dunn was chosen to investigate this serious issue. The university has been asked whether Dunn had the necessary training but has not given a reply. Most of the university community seem to believe that the decision to appoint Dunn was taken with the intention of limiting the damage to the university's reputation.

The university has now accepted that it handled the issue badly and the Vice Chancellor has ordered an enquiry. Perhaps that enquiry will provide the answers which have so far been withheld.

Unhappy Failure

In Britain our universities have considerable discretion and are exposed to little public scrutiny. Universities can make and enforce their own rules; access to students and academics can be firmly controlled; they can tailor the information that is given to persons outside the campus to sustain the view which universities have of themselves, as places of high scholarship and public benefaction.

Universities have changed substantially in the last two decades. They still behave in many respects like scholarly communities but they have expanded rapidly and are now required to market themselves and to compete commercially. As we suggest later, these new expectations seem to have taken priority over the duty of universities to provide a safe place for students and staff to study and work. Sexual harassment and abuse is now commonplace, and this monumental failure has profound consequences. Many thousands of people have suffered harm and distress. In our next chapter we start to tell their story.

2

Stories of Distress

Accurate figures are necessary if we are to develop an effective policy to eliminate sexual abuse. But numbers are only a small part of the story. What affected us most, as we interviewed the victim/survivors, was not how many there are but how much damage was done to their confidence and their lives. As Vera Baird QC, The Victims' Commissioner, said to us,

> "These young women feel diminished."

Each incident of sexual abuse is an appalling personal tragedy.

Their words were heartfelt:

> "I will never fully recover from this."

> "I feel like it is destroying me."

> "It made me distrustful of male friends for a long time afterwards."

> "It was all a living nightmare."

These were comments made to us by four survivors of sexual assault at British universities. One refers to abuse by fellow students, the other three telling us about incidents of sexual assaults on students by members of the teaching staff.

A BBC Investigation into rape, sexual assault and harassment at UK universities found that reports of such incidents had trebled in three years.[1] Louisa (not her real name), raped by a fellow student, is unflinchingly honest about the effect it had on her:

> "I felt that there wasn't really any point in being here because I was just constantly on edge, constantly frightened that he was gonna, like, burst through my bedroom door."

In Chapter 1, we have indicated that the prevalence of such incidents far exceeded our assumption when we began research into this issue.

The cases which have been described to us vary from unwanted sexual comments through to physical assault, including rape. Most of the perpetrators were known to the victim/survivors.

Student Victims and Perpetrators

Let us begin by discussing sexual misconduct and abuse perpetrated by students upon other students.

What follows are some shocking revelations about life for some students in universities, unacknowledged for the most part by the authorities, but presenting daily endurance tests for unfortunate victims of unwanted and unwelcome attention.

In one university, we were told of 18 sexual assault cases of students being assaulted by other students in the past academic year. None had been reported to anyone in authority at the university or the police, although criminal acts were involved.

"Misogyny plays a large part in this", said a University and College Union (UCU) representative. "It is contempt for women".

Over and over again we were told about incidents taking place after sports (particularly rugby) matches, fuelled by large quantities of alcohol. Cheap drink is often available on campus or in pubs targeting students. According to a 2016 report by Universities UK, Durham University is,

> '...strong on sport. Drinking games, often with an element of sexual aggression, are an essential feature of most sports clubs and social societies'.[2]

The police in Durham say that,

> '...cheap drinks and wealthy students make for a toxic cocktail.'[3]

The Bishops' Mill sells entire pitchers of cocktails for just £4.99, while Klute nightclub offers Jägerbombs for £2 and Apple Sourz for £1. Elsewhere a pint costs as little as £1.75. 'Happy Hour' usually extends to at least two hours.[4] Male students, who individually treat their female peers with respect and are considered friends, often behave quite differently in a crowd and under the influence of drink.

> "These boys were my friends – like my brothers. And they destroyed me." (A victim/survivor)

The description in the NUS commissioned report of 2013 is that some men are

> 'Lad by night. Decent guy by day.'[5]

What was described to us by many women as a 'pack mentality' very often seems to take over. Female students are groped, sexually assaulted, abused and, in extreme cases, raped. Sometimes the assaults are public with the perpetrator's mates looking on, encouraging further acts and accompanied by loud jeering.

A union representative in one university told us that,

> "...a girl was peed on when lying on the ground drunk. Friends of the boy standing around laughing."

One woman told us about her shock when a student she knew well,

> "...grabbed me round the waist and then started to touch my breasts and bottom saying, 'you know you want this'".

Students from several universities said that during 'club' nights they expected to be verbally or physically harassed.

> "It is impossible to go on a night out here without being groped."

> "I would expect to be sexually harassed every time I went to one of these clubs."

> "A slap on the arse as a man goes past – and then quickly disappears."

In one of those universities, bouncers are employed by a private security firm who are supposed to 'chuck perpetrators out' but since they often wear headphones to cut out the loud music, they can't hear cries for help!

According to the NUS report, *Hidden Marks*,[6]

> 'Groping, flashing and unwanted sexual comments have become almost "everyday" for some women students'.

Indeed one young woman said to us that, because poor behaviour appears to be more or less accepted,

"It has to be quite bad to even register."

A postgraduate student told us about her experience when, as an undergraduate, she was acting as a volunteer bystander and prepared to intervene in the case of any problems at a college bop. She was called over to the other side of the hall but as she tried to get there,

> "I was met by a circle of eight men who grabbed my breasts and bottom and tried to thrust their hands down my trousers."

One of the most unpleasant accounts we read took place at Durham University where male students played what they called Fat Girl Rodeo:

> 'Spying a pretty girl across a packed night club, the young man in expensive jeans smiles and begins to dance ever closer.
>
> Winking first at his gaggle of grinning chums over her shoulder, he leans in and whispers, "You are hideous" before clamping his arms tightly round her, cuddling her for as long as possible before her struggles force him off.'[7]

At the same university, UUK was told about 'Pull A Pig' evenings among hockey players, where team mates compete to kiss the most 'unattractive woman' on a night out and, chortling, compare notes.[8] It is not difficult to imagine how this affects the abused young woman's self-esteem, and it is hard to get inside the mind of a young man, intelligent enough to have secured a university place, who would behave in such a despicable manner, when he is presumably aware of the damage he is inflicting.

At Warwick University a group of male students wrote the following Facebook messages which were eventually exposed in the Warwick student newspaper, 'The Boar'.

'Sometimes it's fun to go wild and rape 100 girls.'[9]

At one point another Facebook user (also from Warwick) wrote,

> 'Rape her in the street while everybody watches' with another responding, 'It wouldn't be unfair.'

One male student wore a badge with the words:

> 'It's OK to rape on your birthday.'

In 2009, *The Telegraph* reported on 'initiation tests' at a prestigious university organised by sport and drinking clubs for first year students. These usually involve excessive amounts of alcohol and can include 'degrading and depraved (sic) acts' on female students.

So what is going on here?

Why are young men harassing female students with apparent impunity and no remorse?

Why does the problem exist?

Alison Phipps writes about 'the lad culture'[10] which undoubtedly contributes to the generally misogynistic atmosphere reported to us in many universities. (This theme will be pursued in greater detail in Chapter 6.) Drink clearly loosens inhibitions and is given as an excuse for reprehensible behaviour – as if somehow the participants are therefore not answerable for their actions. Many students are living away from restrictions imposed by home and school for the first time in their lives.

One senior lecturer pointed out to us that,

> "...sexual violence is prevalent on the outside so it is not surprising to find it at universities, mirroring the patterns in society."

Another echoed this sentiment, repeating throughout our interview with her that,

> "…colleges and universities do not exist in a vacuum and context is important. We need to consider what is happening outside as well as inside."

Of course both of these observations are true and will be further investigated when we look for solutions in Chapter 8. But blaming what happens in society in general is not a good reason to excuse poor behaviour in institutions of higher education.

The Influence of Pornography

One major factor may be the easy availability of pornography. Many young men carry porn on their phone which they confess to viewing regularly.

These images and videos are easy to access and often boys are watching porn before their first sexual experience. Female degradation in porn is standard, and it is sometimes difficult for young men to know what 'normal' sexual behaviour is. A recent (male) graduate told us that sex, for most men he has listened to when talking about sex, is all about male gratification.

A concerned lecturer in one university said,

> "Porn is everywhere and there has been a case where a student was blatantly watching porn during a lecture."

Her greatest fear is that rape is thus normalised and is the subject of,

> "…jokey discussion and slogans on tee shirts."

A senior staff member said she was very worried about the effect of porn on young men.

> "Porn has become more violent, consent has no place and outlandish behaviour is looked on as normal."

Unfortunately, writes Yomi Adegoke in a piece in *The Guardian* where she interviews a former porn 'star':

> '... a need to appear liberal and open minded has left many modern feminists uncharacteristically quiet on this industry's ethics.'[11]

So a group of people who might be expected to raise concerns about porn have not been vocal on this issue, but it would be wrong just to blame the usual champions of women's rights; we all need to stop being squeamish about this profit-making scandal and speak out about the damage it causes.

The Effect of Single Sex Education on Boys

A theory propounded by some commentators is that in several universities the main male student population comes from single-sex public schools. These boys' contact with females tends to be restricted to mothers and sisters and women in their own immediate social circle. They are unsure about how to approach the opposite sex.

> "They have no idea how to treat girls properly."

Indeed, one man told us that he felt overwhelmed and tongue tied when, coming from a well-known public school, he was suddenly faced with young women in his classes at university.

Lynne Segal says that the effect of single-sex public school education on boys is a 'battering down of emotional responses' and quotes Leonard Woolf who describes what he calls donning 'a male carapace'.[12] Playwright Alan Bennett, returning to Cambridge 63 years after his interview there, recalled:

> 'If the Dons were genial, some of my fellow candidates were less so. That weekend was the first time I had come across public schoolboys in the mass, and I was appalled. They were loud, self-confident... Shouting down the table... while being shockingly greedy. Public school they might be but they were louts.'[13]

The Bullingdon Club is the well-known drinking society at Oxford but in *Posh Boys* Robert Verkaik tells us that Keble College has:

> '...the 'Steamers' whose misogynist antics earned the college the chant, 'We are Keble. We hate women.'[14]

In 1988, Boris Johnson wrote a guide for the best way for aspiring (male) Oxford University politicians to utilise (sic) female students:

> '...Lonely girls from the women's colleges...with their fresh complexions and flowery frocks, they are the prototypes of Conservative Party workers, brisk, stern, running to fat, backing their largely male candidates with a porky decisiveness...'[15]

His remarks were presumably intended to be humorous, but they demonstrate disdain and contempt for female undergraduates.

Alcohol

On social occasions alcohol helps men to bond to cover such feelings of inadequacy. In *The Beer Talking*[16] a researcher recorded conversations between a small group of male university students. They were his friends, and they gave their permission for the recording to take place. His plan was to find out how their attitudes changed as drink allowed them to speak uninhibitedly.

'Their discourse became racist, sexist and homophobic'.

They seemed to distance themselves from feelings of responsibility, covering their anxiety with much loud laughter.

During their increasingly inebriated conversation, 'masculine identity is perpetually achieved, asserted and renegotiated', with constant references to penis size as the defining feature of manhood.

Pejorative language about women coarsened as the evening wore on. Large breasts were referred to as 'Big paps', 'Bag o'puppies', 'Pair of Barratt Houses', 'Mammary batons' and 'Nice set of top bollocks', clearly illustrating their anxiety about and fear of women.[17]

The word 'banter' is frequently used to describe what are considered jocular comments made by boys and men when excusing inappropriate behaviour and jibes. Somehow this is meant to negate the effects of their actions by suggesting that they were only joking, not to be taken seriously and implying that anyone taking offence lacks a sense of humour. They employ this tactic to take the heat out of their aggressive actions. It can render their victims defenceless. Indeed, as Leila Whitely and Tiffany Page tell us,

'Laughter disables other responses.'[18]

Staff Abusing Students

We had originally assumed that most cases of misconduct and abuse would occur among the student population – and indeed we were made aware of many incidents involving only students during our research – but we were taken aback to discover how often we were told about staff who make a deliberate decision to seduce students. A senior university administrator was emphatic when she told us that that these abusive relationships are more traumatic for the victim/survivor than those that take place between students.

In some cases the perpetrators were young tutors but equally prevalent were stories of older, sometimes eminent senior lecturers and professors befriending and then assaulting undergraduates.

An example illustrates the kind of thing we heard repeatedly as we visited various universities in England and Wales.

Ann (not her real name), an undergraduate at a prestigious university, was pursued by a well-known academic with whom she eventually began an affair.

> "He was good looking, charismatic, charming and persuasive. Very appealing to young women", she said, adding: "he needed the constant admiration of younger women".

This description of predators on the staff of universities, from junior lecturers to senior professors, is repeated almost word for word by victim/survivors in the many cases we heard of members of staff abusing students.

A senior lecturer agreed with this description of 'charismatic' tutors.

> "They are adored by students and have an inflated sense of their own significance,"

and then she warned,

> "...but they are tutors not mothers or special friends and can't deliver what they promise."

It is not too hard to understand the attraction of such men to an 18-year-old, possibly far from home, perhaps unsure or lonely and anxious to please.

> "Students seek social acceptance and are finding their place in the university."

Typically, these young and vulnerable women are deliberately targeted and groomed by predators. The staff member engages his victims in intellectual conversations, continues with more personal chat, probing to find any weaknesses or problems they may have, and then plays at being, 'the senior sympathetic figure'. As part of their seduction technique, these men suggest further private meetings/tutorials in a pub or café away from the university campus, sometimes even offering gifts. All of this is clearly flattering to a perhaps naïve young woman who understandably enjoys this special attention.

As one union representative said to us:

> "You want to feel grown up. So if you are 'dating' a lecturer that is a special relationship to boast about."

> 'The lecture hall provides a stage and the male academic is there with all the cultural and social signs and symbols.'[19]

So when such men say, 'I chose you', sometimes the young women naively boast about what they see as their conquests.

Because students have reached the age of 18, they are considered to be consenting adults and the power differential between them and the staff member is ignored. We were told that,

> "...the most vulnerable female undergraduates are bright, attractive and well-motivated young women who enjoy engaging intellectually during seminars."

One university teacher when questioned about this situation told a researcher:

> 'We have few perks in this job without denying us these rights.'[20]

Another academic was described to us as,

> "...rampant, as he is always after students and staff."

We were told of a married senior lecturer who asked a student to meet him at his house and when she arrived he answered the door in his underpants.

We heard of university lecturers grading new female students on their looks (1–10) and then deliberately grooming the ones they feel are most attractive. They even pointed out to their interested male colleagues, students who may be more to their taste.

No doubt most of the predators think that they are keeping their activities secret but some are well known throughout their university. One senior academic told us:

> "We know who they are. They particularly like to go to conferences attended by young women. We do our best to block them by turning down their applications and rejecting their papers."

The perpetrators are often married and end the relationship with the student after a few months, leaving her isolated, bewildered, often blaming herself and not knowing to whom to turn for support. That is what happened to Ann. In the end she decided to continue with her studies, but according to an NUS report[21] many young women caught up in such cases lose confidence, their attendance suffers and they eventually leave.

We heard a number of examples:

"I lost interest in my course, a loss of motivation."

Those who stay on remain fearful of chance encounters with their abuser:

"Places can trigger feelings of fear."

"I avoid places on campus where he might go," said one survivor.

"My heart thumps every time I have to go near that building", said another.

A student who told her story to Leila White and Tiffany Page,

'...described herself as afraid but also immobilised.'[22]

In this kind of case the student is often mistrusted by her peers, even ostracised. They suspect that if she achieves high grades, her results may be connected to her relationship with the staff member. She does not even tell her parents when the relationship ends, fearing their opprobrium. She is left coping on her own with her self-esteem in tatters.

At St. Hugh's College, Oxford, the Governing Body decided that sexual relations between teaching staff and their students should be prohibited.

It was refreshing to hear what Elish Angiolini, Principal of St. Hugh's and a former Lord Advocate of Scotland, says as part of her welcome speech to new students.

"You have come here to study and to have a wonderful time. Do not cause a catastrophe by not understanding what consent is about. If your tutor attempts to initiate a sexual relationship with you, do not respond. However 'gorgeous' you think your tutor is, if you start a sexual relationship with them, you will be out of here and they will be dismissed." [23]

At St Hugh's, consent training is obligatory for all new students

Higher Grades in Degrees Offered in Exchange for Sex

All of this has a long history. In Harriet Harman's autobiographical book, *A Woman's Work*,[24] she describes how her tutor, T.V. Sathyamurthy, called her in to discuss her final degree.

> 'He told me that I was borderline between a 2:1 and a 2:2 but that if I had sex with him it would definitely be a 2:1... I had no hesitation in repelling his advances. (Despite rejecting him I got a 2:1).'

We heard similar stories from other women, one of whom did consent to this blackmail, got the required result but has bitterly regretted her compliance ever since.

It is sometimes said that female students themselves offer sex to tutors in exchange for a higher final grade. In fact in all our interviews we only heard of one such example; an undergraduate, who told friends that she had set her sights on a particular married lecturer whom she was determined to seduce. She succeeded, boasting about her conquest in emails to friends, got the grades she wanted and seemed utterly unrepentant. Other women are not so lucky.

Unkind comments shared on social media add to the misery of the victim of abuse. Reaction from staff and students, we were told, varies from,

> "Excitement, pleasure in gossip and titillation to those who were horrified, felt uncomfortable..."

Damaging Relationships

Incidents of sexual abuse are often reported and discussed on social media, with students taking sides. This generalises and magnifies the problem.

A (male) teacher at one university said that he knew of,

> "...two female students who had left in the past year because they could not tolerate the atmosphere of harassment."

Academics in close relationships with students are often keen to protect their own position. The most bizarre reaction we heard about was of a staff member who had an affair with a third year student. When she applied for a post, having been given a glowing reference by her personal tutor, she did not get the job because the reference from her former lover was so poor. When asked about his motives he replied,

> "I didn't want to show her any favouritism."

An angry senior lecturer said bitterly:

> "The role of tutors is to support students not to view them as possible sexual partners".

An interesting perspective was offered by a sensitive male university teacher, whose courses are female dominated. He told us that he was glad that most doors have glass panels.

Field Trips

Field and research trips can be hazardous,

> "...because some men regard them as an opportunity to behave badly and have casual affairs."

We were told of one woman who lived in a caravan while researching in a rather remote area. She was approached by her male supervisor who pestered her, asking to be invited in, finally only leaving her alone when she told him that she had a fiancé.

However, she felt very vulnerable throughout the field trip in these circumstances.

Some people talk as if the experience of sexual harassment and abuse fades quickly. This was not what we found when we listened to the stories of victim/survivors. The pain is strong and persistent.

The oldest case we heard about, and by far the most distressing, was that of a woman, now herself a senior university lecturer, who contacted us to talk about the abuse she suffered many years ago. This proves how long term the effects can be.

This is her story.

She was studying comparative religion and spent six months overseas. The university gave her no prior fieldwork training, briefing or advice, and she felt very lonely and isolated in a country far from home where she did not speak the language. Her mentor was the only person she knew there – an extremely eminent religious man and an admired professor who invited her into his study soon after she arrived.

> "I was young and naïve and assumed that I was about to have an academic and spiritual conversation with this devout man."

After asking her to sit next to him on the sofa he plied her with drink.

> "He chatted and I drank."

He then started to push and kiss her. She tried to push him off at first. He called her 'boring' and persisted. She realised that she was trapped:

> "Where am I going to run? I don't know how to call the police in this country and there is no-one to shout for."

She froze and he raped her.

In that moment she made, as she put it, 'survival-based decision to consent'. In the end she continued to be sexually abused by him over a period of six months. Having consented once, she felt she had no basis to withdraw that consent. In any case, he said he would kill her if she told anyone and he would destroy her career. She felt totally powerless.

She returned to the UK profoundly traumatised but had no woman to turn to. Her Head of Department was male, and when she told him what had happened, she was offered a private apology, but there was no investigation or sanction of the perpetrator. In an understatement she said to us:

> "I can look back on that experience of reporting and I think the university did not do enough."

The idea that she had 'consented' troubled her for 13 years and was only dealt with after more than two years of intensive counselling.

She asked us, when we wrote about her story, to stress the psychological effect on victims,

> "You feel as if you are partly to blame. It can be very hard to see that this is absolutely not the case."

This brave woman is adamant that her story should be told:

> "I would like the equivalent of the negativity that happened to me to be turned into positivity", she said, adding:

> "We know much more now than we did then about the psychological reasons why victims don't come forward and why we wrongly assume the blame. If things are going to change, now is the time."

PhD Students

PhD students and younger staff members are particularly vulnerable. Both rely on their supervisor or Head of Department for references.

PhD students often have only one supervisor. A great deal is at stake for them in this relationship: expert knowledge and guidance from their mentor, by whom their thesis may also be assessed. Their future careers depend on an encouraging reference from this person. The power differential is clear and crossing the line to a more intimate relationship is very risky. On the other hand, if they refuse the advances of this senior member of staff, they could be jeopardizing their whole career.

Venki Ramakrishnan, scientist and President of the Royal Society, was asked on the Desert Island Discs programme[25] about reports of a culture of bullying in Science.

He said that he did not know the extent of the bullying because,

> '...a lot of the incidents are anecdotal'.

However, he then added:

> 'I think the problem comes from the enormous power differential. Very often the supervisor controls the student's funding and it might even be paid from the supervisor's own grant. The other source of power is more subtle. If the student wants to get on in their career they always need a reference from their supervisor. Even a luke-warm reference can sink the prospects of a student.'

Although this story relates to bullying in one academic sphere, it is not hard to imagine how much more vulnerable a student might feel if they report an incident of sexual abuse by their supervisor.

Several women said that their supervisors took every opportunity to intrude into their space:

> "He leant over me – too close,"

was a common complaint, particularly when looking at something on a computer.

We were told by a former very senior staff member that when she was a junior lecturer her boss would manufacture the need for one to one meetings, patting his desk and saying, 'sit here'. He would stand too close and keep asking her to look at the computer screen in his office, encouraging her to bend over to see it more clearly.

A junior academic told us about her experience as a PhD student with,

> "…a very renowned supervisor."

One day, out of the blue, the supervisor said she needed (sic) to go away for a weekend with him.

> "I tried to brush him off and spoke to a colleague about it. I could have reported him but was not aware of procedures to do so. And anyway that would have meant the end of my career with no references and no job ever."

She never met him again. She finished her PhD but felt that the subsequent intellectual level of support was not satisfactory.

In this case, as in so many others we heard of, the reputation of this man was known but excused:

> "He's just an old fashioned guy."

> "We know what he is like."

"It's just Andy being Andy."

"Oh it's just a young man's shenanigans."

Or the warnings:

"He has a reputation as a bit of a lech."

"Beware of that guy."

Another PhD student who succumbed to the advances of her supervisor described him to us as,

"…initially charming though narcissistic, then controlling and sexually demanding."

We were told of a senior lecturer who met a female former PhD student at a conference some years after she had left the university where a professor had been reported for preying on younger women. This man's name came up in conversation and the former student burst into tears asking,

"Is he here? He was one of my supervisors and made my life a misery with his sexual demands."

To counter this problem, in some universities it is now stipulated that a PhD student has to have two supervisors.

Junior Academic Staff

Junior staff members can also be preyed upon by senior colleagues. They are dependent on the goodwill of their line manager, who is often a professor valued by the university.

We have been told about sexual assaults on women who have worked with the abuser for some years and had no reason to expect a sexual attack.

In a previous book[26] we interviewed and were given full permission to write about an assault on a junior lecturer by her boss – a senior and respected professor whom she had known for years.

> 'Caroline (not her real name) went to see her boss in his new office, as arranged, to discuss her research. When the conversation came to an end, he asked her to look out of the window, which she did, thinking he was asking her to admire the view from his first floor window.'

That was when he attacked her,

> "…launching himself from behind, putting his hands under my arms and grabbing my breasts. I kept shouting 'Get off me, get off me', trying to prise his hands off my body… He eventually backed off."

She described it as, 'a frenzied attack'.

She told no one for a while, 'feeling utterly ashamed' and asking herself,

> "Have I been sending out the wrong signals?"

This reaction after the incident is extremely common. We heard the same words from several victim/survivors. Were they in some way to blame? This feeling is then followed by a desire to hide and wipe the whole thing from their mind. In some cases this leads to a delay in reporting the matter. But even when they do act, however swiftly, the incident can affect their well-being, their security and their relationships both current and future.

Elish Angiolini QC, Principal of St. Hugh's College, Oxford, speaking from her long experience in the justice system, told us that,

> "...the reactions to being sexually assaulted are unique and often differ from responses to other crimes and this is often not understood. The distress is so great that in reality, the vast majority of victims never disclose."

A young academic from a strict West Indian church background, described how, in her first job, one man in particular made her feel uncomfortable, always commenting on what she was wearing. She asked him to stop, saying:

> "I come here to work. I do not ask for compliments"

He ignored this and then there was an incident when a telephone rang in the staff room and she reached across to answer it. He came across and,

> "...grabbed me and touched me. I froze."

She told her (female) team leader who was sympathetic but said:

> "We know what he's like."

The general effect of this has caused this young woman to be guarded and to keep her distance in relationships.

She feels at an added disadvantage, making a telling remark:

> "I do not want to be seen as the angry black woman."

Some victim/survivors say that they do not report because they do not know whether the incident is serious enough or even whether they will be believed.

That is, of course, if they know how/to whom to report and many people told us that the reporting procedures are not well-publicised.

Overwhelming Feelings of Guilt and Shame

It is evidently risky for a junior lecturer to make a serious complaint against an often well-known and academically respected senior staff member. The university's reputation is at stake in these circumstances, and the complainant is likely to find herself thwarted by those in authority. As we will see in Chapter 7, with universities struggling with their cash flow, they are reluctant to allow the reputation of a leader in his field being impugned. We were told,

> "He brings money in so he is inviolate".

Two women, both lecturers at the same university, told us of a man they described as a long-standing well-known professor, who not only targeted academics but also PhD students and undergraduates.

When both women found that he had been in a relationship with one of them while attempting to press himself on the other during the same period, they also discovered that he had been banned from field trips in the past because of an incident with a student.

They took action against him and won, even though friends of his put in a statement which he used in his defence.

The accused was found guilty.

But as one of the woman ruefully said,

> "It has probably damaged our careers."

It is not just students and other academics who are at risk of assault. Other staff are also vulnerable.

A worried academic told us of his Head of Department under whom 'a heavily macho culture' became the norm.

> "Drinking was a social requirement and so was a deep interest in sport."

Parties occurred regularly and on one social occasion the department head came up behind one of the secretaries and grabbed her breasts.

This incident was reported and the perpetrator was banned from the main area where the secretaries worked. However, he subsequently successfully applied for a prestigious post in another university, even though, it transpired, they already knew about his predatory reputation. 'We know everything', was their response when a person telephoned to warn his new colleagues.

> "They (universities) want to hold on to their stars",

was the weary reaction of another lecturer.

Under Reporting

As we demonstrate in Chapter 5, the procedures for complaints to be made are either unknown to victims, difficult to locate or understand, involving in some cases, lengthy and tortuous processes and several meetings with possibly unsympathetic administrators.

Sanctions, if applied, seem paltry. A union representative told us that often the complainant is simply advised thus:

> "Well don't eat in that area," or, "don't walk alone in the car park."

We were told that,

> "...advice for new students is 'pretty inaccessible, turgid and hard to follow,'"

In one university, processes were described to us as,

"...procedural idiosyncrasy ... shrouded in mystery."

It is not surprising therefore that complaints are comparatively rare.

More than one victim/survivor who spoke to us said that they did not report because they did not think the assault was serious enough.

Victims also say that they are reluctant to complain if the perpetrator is a member of their friendship group: they are concerned about the consequences, both to the accused and themselves. There is a feeling among some victim/survivors that if they make a complaint they somehow 'lose control' of the situation.

We heard that when one victim decided to proceed by taking her case against an abusive member of the teaching staff to a higher authority, she was told:

> "Do you want to make a formal complaint? If so I have to warn you that it might be difficult for you and might cost him his job."

With this kind of advice it is not surprising that formal complaints seem to be sparse.

As we were told by one victim/survivor:

> "It's not necessarily the severity of the incident that is the problem, but you have to think if you are strong enough to deal with the consequences of reporting."

The victim does not want to be seen as a trouble maker. And being a nuisance is clearly how some universities seem to regard complainants. As a senior lecturer said tartly:

> "The attitude is – we want to get rid of the problem so we'll get rid of the student."

> "It's easier to get kicked out for plagiarism than for assaulting women",

was the wry opinion of a former Student Union representative.

Some do not want to make a complaint because they simply want to forget about the whole incident. Some feel complicit – wondering whether they inadvertently sent out encouraging signals.

Other survivors, for various reasons, do not want the abuser to be punished. This is particularly true where the perpetrator is a member of the teaching staff. They do not want to be responsible for possibly damaging his career.

Some universities have a reputation as a 'liberal' environment, and several people we interviewed said that there is a notion that to do anything like complaining would be to interfere with what was described to us as the,

> "…unstructured free expression of will (sic)."

But one tutor asked rather desperately,

> "What message are you giving if you think this is alright? It undermines us as women. They are protecting the university rather than the student."

Understanding the Distress

At a conference on sexual misconduct in universities we were told that the most poignant contributions came from two survivors who had radically different feelings about recounting their ordeal:

> "Am I making it worse by speaking about it?",

asked one, while the other said:

> "It has given me my voice back".

We were told by one of those responsible for arranging the conference that these two women had more impact on delegates, many of whom were university administrators and other staff, than any other contributors.

To explain what being a victim is really like, we tell the story of Karli.

Karli

Karli Wagener, an undergraduate from Germany studying at Leicester University, has bravely waived her right to anonymity after being raped by a fellow student.

Her story was published in *The Times*,[27] and we can now add what she subsequently told us about the details of her ordeal and its aftermath.

Karli is a proficient sportswoman, captain of the volleyball team, and after a celebratory party she was escorted home by a committee member of another university sports club. Arriving at her house he pleaded to come inside to get warm and then said,

> "You owe me a kiss. He then pushed me back, held me by the throat. I blacked out and when I came round he was on top of me, raping me."

Afterwards she was in a lot of pain, 'I felt ripped apart', but, accompanied by a friend, she immediately went to the police. The detectives to whom she spoke were very understanding. She went back to Germany for a while and on her return to Leicester contacted Amy Moran, the President of the Student Union, 'who was enormously supportive', and they started a campaign at the university.

Unfortunately, the only action taken by the university was the sanction imposed by the disciplinary panel that her abuser should not be allowed to make any contact with her.

She told us that she

> "finds it difficult to sleep, keeps doubting herself and feels unworthy."

For a while she found it very hard to concentrate for any length of time.

> "I can talk about it but my body is still in shock. I did not want to believe that someone would do such a thing to me. My mind doesn't want to accept it."

Karli has contributed to a Radio 4 podcast[28] about her experience. Four students from other universities also participated, including a male student who had been raped at university, and it is an indication of their distress that the recording which had been scheduled to last two hours actually took five.

However, a positive result has been that the campaign at Leicester University against abuse is proving successful.

The Student Union successfully fought for a ban on the man accused by Karli of entering the campus unless he is attending timetabled classes. He has also been told that he must actively avoid meeting her.

During Freshers' week, posters advertising the university #Metoo campaign were put up over the campus and all new students are given much more information about sexual harassment and assault. Since the campaign began, the university has recruited five more trauma counsellors to their well-being service.

Mental Health

We were alarmed and saddened by the stories we were told of assault and even rape and by the damage suffered by the victims.

Surely no one starting at university, full of optimism and with expectations of new and interesting pathways opening up, should be subjected to the kind of treatment which undermines their confidence and lowers their self-esteem.

PhD students and junior staff members should not have to worry about fending off unwanted overtures from their senior colleagues or even feel forced into granting sexual favours, in order to protect their careers.

Hidden Marks, the NUS nationwide report on sexual harassment and abuse suffered by women students in universities, gives a detailed account of the

> 'impact of stalking, violence and sexual assault on women students'.[29]

Their survey showed that most respondents spoke of a deterioration in mental health; their relationships were affected; and they considered leaving their course. They admitted to increased fear, avoiding the perpetrator, a loss of interest and motivation. Some moved house and were frightened of going out alone

> 'I feel that this is slowly destroying me.'

In September 2019, Sir Norman Lamb MP published information obtained from 110 universities under Freedom of Information requests on the demand and support in mental health for their students.

Many universities had no record of help needed, although some – like Bristol, Kingston, Sussex, Cambridge and Northumbria – were taking their responsibility seriously. Many said that, given their limited resources, they could not deal with mental health alone. They needed cooperation from parents and budgets to install new systems. At the moment the average waiting time to be seen by health professionals is 43 days. Sir Norman said:

> 'We know that there have been some tragedies among some student populations – students who have taken their own lives. If that happens while they are waiting for support, that is utterly intolerable. Students ... have every reason to expect a duty of care from their universities.'[30]

We are glad that action has been taken at London's Brunel University. Julia Buckingham, Vice Chancellor and President of Brunel and also President of UUK, told us that students at Brunel are invited to say, at the point of registration, if they would like a named person to be contacted by the university if there is concern about their mental health and safety. Approximately 80% opted into this suggestion.

Universities have to solve this serious problem. It is their responsibility to ensure that justice is done. As Vera Baird, the Victim's Commissioner, says,

> "Universities cannot outsource their duty of care."[31]

3

Doubts and Discontent

A victim of sexual abuse needs to be believed, supported and well-advised. That is the very least that a university should manage. Unfortunately the experience of many students and junior staff is that universities often fail to meet even these modest requirements.

> "My friends said that I ought to report what had happened, but when I did, the advisor gave me a lot of reasons why I should think again and not take it any further."

The speaker is a first year undergraduate who said she had been sexually assaulted by another student. She insisted that she did not get the sympathy and kindness she needed.

Others told a similar story.

> "When I went to university, I thought that I would be looked after. I was shocked that when I was in trouble they did not seem to think what had happened to me was important."

Many of the victim/survivors who spoke to us were extremely bitter. At first they were bewildered by the university's rather passive reaction to their complaint. But as time passed and little was done, frustration turned to anger.

> "They did not seem to be listening to what I was telling them."

And a truly awful comment:

> "Being raped was dreadful but the way I was treated afterwards upset me even more. I think it was all the hoops I had to jump through that caused my PTSD."

A Surprising Consensus

In our research we collected views from all parts of the university community. We interviewed students, academics at all levels, support staff from many departments, trade union representatives, NUS and Student Union office holders, specialists, advisors and managers.

We expected to find a variety of opinions ranging from people who believed that the existing systems fell short of what was needed through to people who were more satisfied with what universities are doing. Instead, we found a surprising level of consensus. Over and over again we heard that the present arrangements are not working and that a new approach is urgently needed. Significantly, not a single interviewee told us that universities are doing enough.

There were, of course, differences in emphasis. The most optimistic assessments came from senior managers. Some pointed to recent initiatives which they regarded as encouraging. A few sought to explain the universities' current failures by suggesting that universities were reflecting the culture of Britain as a whole.

> "It happens throughout British society so it is not surprising that sexual misconduct also happens in universities."

Nevertheless, without exception every manager acknowledged that universities had, as one put it, 'to up their game'.

Other groups were more severe in their criticism. A dominant view amongst staff and students is that, whatever Vice Chancellors say in public, most universities are reluctant to get to grips with the problem of sexual harassment and abuse. Indeed one senior academic insisted that, on the contrary,

> "...they do everything possible to distance themselves from the issue"

An administrator, who has sometimes been given the task of investigating complaints, thought that only the most serious sexual assaults get the full attention of senior management. The innuendoes, the sexual 'jokes', the verbal abuse, the touching, the patting and the unwanted sexual advances – all of which are deeply upsetting to the victim – tend to be brushed aside. She said that the attitude of management is usually:

> "Nothing much happened, so let's move on."

We heard one phrase many times.

> "They (the university authorities) don't really want to know."

The Zellick Legacy

Universities have a duty of care to their staff and students, so it is disheartening that they are now accused of neglect or worse by the very people whom they should be protecting. How this came about is partly explained by bad decisions taken, albeit under pressure, over 25 years ago.

The sad story began in 1992 when a student named Austen Donellan was suspended by King's College, London, after being accused of rape by another student. The case went to court and Donellan was found not guilty. He then took legal action against the university and won substantial damages.[1]

This development caused great anxiety to universities throughout Britain. A Taskforce, chaired by Graham Zellick, President of Queen Mary and Westfield College, was set up to recommend how universities should handle disciplinary cases, and particularly cases of sexual violence and abuse. The Taskforce produced extensive guidance which came to be known as the Zellick Principles.[2]

The Taskforce's core advice was that a university should never investigate a complaint of sexual assault or rape; that is a matter for the police. This embargo should be maintained even if both parties want an internal investigation, and even if the complainant has no intention of reporting the matter to the police. The Zellick Taskforce left no room for doubt.

> 'Internal action for rape and sexual assault is out of the question'.[3]

Should the university take the initiative and report the complaint to the police? This is also ruled out in most cases:

> '…only in exceptional circumstances should the university report an alleged crime to the police contrary to the wishes of the victim.'[4]

What are these exceptional circumstances? The advice of the Taskforce was robust.

> Only, 'when it appears significant violence has been used which exposes others to danger, or where there have been similar allegations in the past which likewise suggest a risk to other persons'.[5]

Some apologists have suggested that the Zellick Taskforce was merely encouraging universities to be careful in handling allegations of sexual abuse, but this is disingenuous. Zellick made a strong recommendation to universities not to institute an immediate internal inquiry into rape or sexual assault under any circumstances. If the matter was referred to the police, no internal action should be taken until the police had completed their inquiries. And if the matter was not referred to the police, no internal action should take place because it was inappropriate for universities to investigate such matters.

The Zellick Principles did what the Taskforce intended. They conditioned university behaviour. The Taskforce's wording was unambiguous and the subtext, although unstated, was obvious: remember Austen Donellan's legal action against King's College and keep as far away from sexual abuse cases as possible. This was the message which, in one form or another, was written into university procedures. Non-intervention, or as little intervention as possible, became the way universities normally responded to allegations of sexual abuse. It was a mistaken and miserable policy which has caused distress and harm to very many people.

Zellick held sway for more than two decades. At last, in 2016, with criticism growing inexorably, UUK decided that the Zellick Principles had to be reviewed. A report was prepared by Nicola Bradfield from solicitors Pinsent Masons, assisted by a UUK steering group. Dame Janet Beer, at that time President of UUK, has subsequently spoken of this report as replacing Zellick.[6] Unfortunately the situation is more complicated and less encouraging than she suggests.

Drafted by a solicitor, the new review does not take as its starting point the university's duty of care for its staff and students – which we believe should be the primary consideration – but, like Zellick, focuses on how universities can avoid legal risk. It follows the Zellick Taskforce in advising universities to take no action if a matter is in the hands of the police. This usually means a delay of very many months in dealing with a complaint of sexual harassment or abuse and ignores the fact that the police do not object to a university taking action in respect of a breach of its own rules while the police are investigating whether a criminal act has been committed.

Nevertheless, there is some progress. Universities are reassured that if a complaint is not referred to the police, an internal inquiry can take place. At least this gets rid of the blanket embargo which the Zellick Taskforce recommended. However, in trying to explain the extent of this new freedom, the report seems to lose its bearings. The report's primary concern is the acute problem of sexual abuse but the authors decide, in extraordinary fashion, to illuminate the issue by referring to much less serious breaches of regulations.

> 'By way of example, taking a library book without permission and drawing graffiti on a university building may constitute the criminal offences of theft and criminal damage and disciplinary offences of taking property belonging to the university without permission and causing damage to university property.'[7]

This passage in the report is seriously misjudged. Universities need to persuade their staff and students that sexual abuse is taken very seriously. But statements of good intent will not carry much conviction if universities imply that a complaint of sexual abuse can be viewed in the same way as the unauthorised removal of a library book.

In any event it is unlikely that the improvement suggested in the Pinsent Mason review will have much early effect. We show in

Chapter 5 that the Zellick Principles are still deeply embedded in many university procedures. Moreover, university administrators and HR professionals have operated on a hands-off basis for a generation; they will not change their long-held practices overnight. Worse still, the new guidelines are not mandatory and the task of reviewing and amending university policies and procedures to reflect the recommended changes will be arduous. Dame Janet Beer is an optimist but Sarah Green of the End Violence Against Women Coalition is far more circumspect.

> '... while these intentions are good, UUK do not propose any mechanism for enforcement, monitoring is left to individual institutions and there are no recommendations to government for a change in the law should universities not comply with the recommendations.'[8]

From our examination of existing procedures, we believe that progress is likely to be slow and cautious and rather than urgent and committed.

Capacity

Even if universities decide on a radical change in their approach to sexual abuse, they will be inhibited by a shortage of expertise. We were surprised to be told by so many of our interviewees that universities are trying to deal with this complex problem in a manner which seems very amateurish, without specialist knowledge and without sufficient trained staff. One manager said that there are

> "...very few people with the responsibility for reducing sexual abuse and they often have limited experience. They act in isolation without the opportunity to link up and increase their impact."

One result is that many universities have little understanding of sexual abuse, either its nature or its origins. Only about 20 universities have recruited a fully trained specialist to be their advisor. That leaves over 80 universities in England and Wales who rely on personnel in the Student Services Section and on volunteers from the academic staff and from the Student Union. It is often the case that fewer than 20 persons have this responsibility in a university with 20,000 or 30,000 students. Most volunteers have received only rudimentary training and provide advisory and support work in addition to their normal duties. The verdict of one professional is harsh.

> "This is a function which relies on well-meaning part-timers."

We asked whether universities used the knowledge of academics in Gender Studies and related departments to assist in the design of policy and practice. We found few instances where this was happening. One senior academic said that she knew of several female academics who took a personal interest in the issue and we interviewed some of those who were named. We found that, like so many others, they are frustrated at the slow pace of reform. They are full of ideas but their suggestions are rarely welcome. Senior management seems to regard these women as over-critical outsiders rather than as potential partners in the pursuit of reform.

Universities are meant to value specialist knowledge based on research and analysis. So it is strange that very many universities are reluctant to recruit the necessary expertise to tackle a problem which, unless properly addressed, can cause such damage and hardship. As we demonstrate elsewhere, there are many myths about the causes and nature of sexual abuse. Without specialist advice it is highly likely that policy initiatives will be based on false assumptions and that resources deployed to deal with sexual abuse will be mis-directed.

When we asked why so few specialists have been recruited, the answer usually focused on the cost. Yet employing a full-time specialist would require only a tiny part of the budget of even the smallest university. Failure to invest in these essential skills suggests that many university managers do not appreciate the seriousness of the problem and are not giving it the right level of importance.

Reputation

When explaining university priorities, many of our interviewees told us that the over-riding concern of university managers is the reputation of the university. Higher education is now a highly competitive business and universities want to attract students and financial support, including research funding, partnership money and sponsorship. So a high priority is given to presentation and public relations. One academic claimed that his university had,

> "…more people in the PR department than in Classics and History."

This seemed an extraordinary claim but we checked and we found that he was nearly right. History had a few more but Classics had less.

Nevertheless, a concern for the university's reputation does not explain the relatively low priority accorded to sexual abuse. After all, the knowledge that a particular university has a high incidence of sexual abuse must surely damage that university's reputation. What we were told in response to this objection was unexpected.

We had assumed that the best way to avoid the reputational damage associated with sexual harassment and abuse would be to deal with the problem in an expert and rigorous manner: less sexual abuse will reduce the risk of a public scandal. To our surprise we were told that many universities take a different approach. Their way of avoiding reputational damage is to do nothing which alerts the public (including potential students, funders, journalists and politicians) to the fact that sexual harassment and abuse is taking place in their university. Apparently, a news blackout is sometimes regarded as preferable to facing the problem head-on.

We learned just how far some universities go to avoid any open discussion of sexual matters. One Student Union representative said that her university always wanted to talk about conduct and behaviour in a general way rather than being upfront and talking about sexual misconduct and sexual abuse. She said that the university believed that even,

> "...having a well-publicised sexual harassment policy is tantamount to admitting that sexual harassment is taking place."

This seemed an extreme example but people from several other universities confirmed that managers were reluctant to focus on sexual misconduct and even, in some cases, avoid getting involved in discussion about anything to do with sex.

This bizarre finding was reinforced by a number of Student Union representatives who told us that senior managers are keen that discussions about sexual abuse take place between the Student Union and the department which supervises student services and not at meetings with senior management. One said that the attitude is,

> "Please go and talk about it somewhere else."

Involving the Student Union and the trade unions is very sensible but if their point of contact is not with senior managers but with managers lower down the hierarchy, frustration will soon result. This form of delegation means, in effect, that sexual abuse is being given a lower position on the university's policy agenda. Unless senior managers are involved, there might be a good deal of discussion and perhaps even some encouraging words, but early action is unlikely.

Although it was put to us that this reluctance to spend time discussing sexual abuse is driven by PR and policy considerations, other testimony suggests that more personal considerations might also be important. Most of the top jobs in universities are held by men. A lot of them do not seem able to talk about modern day sexual mores with much confidence. The point was summed up vividly by one experienced academic:

> "It is very hard for a 60 year old man to talk convincingly about the lifestyle of 18 year old girls."

She had noticed male managers looking embarrassed when sexual matters were discussed. Many older men clearly do not know the vocabulary and seem worried that they might say something which would be embarrassing or sound stupid.

> "When we move on to discuss other matters there is an obvious sense of relief."

A young man whom we interviewed added a further explanation. At a recent conference he was shocked at the resentment shown by the older male speakers. They knew that times have changed and that behaviour which was quite common in their youth is no longer tolerated. Nevertheless they complained about new legislation on harassment and many clearly thought that things had gone too far. He said that the public face of his university was of a liberally minded and modern institution. However, he made clear that this is only part of the truth. Many older men clearly do not believe in the need for further reform.

Another academic suggested that there might be another personal reason for a reluctance to get into the details of sexual harassment and abuse. She reminded us that, when men who are now senior in the university establishment were undergraduates and junior academics, much of what is now regarded as sexual misconduct was thought of as innocent flirting and overtly sexual remarks were dismissed as 'banter'. She suggested that when they hear details of what some male student is said to have done, their first reaction is probably:

> "There but for the grace of God go I."

Illusions

The practice of avoidance, whatever its basis, is often accompanied by a suggestion that the problem of sexual abuse is being greatly exaggerated. One woman, who was pressing for urgent action, said that she was told by a senior manager that she was,

> "...in the grip of the #MeToo movement."

A union representative said that, faced with a man in denial, she painstakingly explained that sexual abuse is a country-wide problem and no university is immune. But he would have none of it. He kept repeating what was evidently a personal mantra.

> "We don't have any of that here."

This is a dangerous illusion that can only be sustained because a tiny proportion of incidents are reported to the university. Elsewhere we explore the reasons for under-reporting in greater detail but, according to our interviewees, a significant part of the explanation is that victims of sexual abuse do not want to expose themselves to the scrutiny and publicity that reporting might involve.

> "No one who has been assaulted wants to re-live the experience over and over again."

Significantly, when a university introduces anonymous reporting, the number of complaints of sexual abuse increases considerably. In one large university we were told that the numbers went up five-fold. But even so, insiders say that the university is still hearing about only a small proportion of the incidents which take place.

Low levels of reporting help sustain another comforting illusion. Each incident can be regarded as a 'regrettable aberration' which does not require the leadership of the university to modify its convenient view that the institution is a safe place to work and study. The unwillingness of universities to accept that the problem of sexual abuse is pervasive frustrated many of our interviewees.

> "Abuse is rife in this university but management will not accept that."

The way universities approach the problem is said to be mistaken.

> "Every incident is treated as a one-off. They won't see that the problem is deep-seated."

A student who acted as a senior representative in her Student Union was even more direct.

> "We had four rapes in two days and the college still behaved as if we did not have a serious problem."

Reporting

Some students and staff detected more than a little hypocrisy in their university's approach.

> "They say that all incidents should be reported but then make it very difficult for anyone to put a report in."

We asked one academic in a prestigious university whether his students knew how to report an incident of sexual abuse. He said that there was,

> "…some sort of guidance for new students telling them how to contact Student Union reps, but I do not know of any concrete information to help students make a report."

Another more senior academic told us of her difficulty in giving effective advice to students who have suffered abuse.

> "There are procedures in place in (this university) but none of them functions successfully."

Several students told us that they did not know how to report abuse. Often they went to their tutor but then found that this was not the correct starting point.

> "I told my tutor what had happened and thought things would be followed up. But when I asked how far my complaint had got, I was told that I had only raised it informally and, if I wanted it investigated, I would have to put it all in writing."

Poor communications make things worse. A number of the more progressive universities have introduced an initiative called *Report and Support* which is intended to simplify the reporting process. However, this new facility is not always well-publicised. One union representative found that the university HR department was telling students and staff that complaints could not be recorded unless complainants gave their names. When the union representative challenged this rule at a university seminar she was surprised to be told by the speaker that, because the university had adopted the *Report and Support* programme, anonymous reporting was now possible. Both the Union representative and the HR department insist that they had not been informed of the change.

An academic from another university many miles away told us that this failure was quite common.

> "Most of the procedures are invisible. They are not communicated and are difficult to find. It is a mess."

Complex

Those students who managed to find the correct procedures, expressed surprise that they are so complicated.

> "I wanted to know what to do and I had to work my way through fifteen pages that were very difficult to understand."

One victim/survivor complained that the Student Complaints procedure,

> "…wasn't just about sexual harassment. It covered everything. There were great long sections on the use of IT equipment and on accommodation."

Another said that she was frightened by the suggestion in the procedure that she should try to sort matters out with the man who was harassing her.

> "I didn't want to go near him. The advisor told me that I could ignore that part but it was all written down in the procedure. There was even the suggestion of going to mediation if I did not want to see him on my own."

After struggling through these difficulties, victim/survivors thought that they would be kept informed of what was going on. We heard many complaints that this often does not happen. We were told of one university where, once disciplinary action is considered, it becomes a matter of policy not to involve the person making the complaint.

> "It is the investigator who reports to the disciplinary committee and, if it goes further, to a committee of the Senate. The complainant does not appear, which might be considered a kindness, but no-one tells her what the outcome is. The complainant's involvement ends with an interview by the investigator."

We were told that the HR department of one university was refusing to tell a complainant the result of the disciplinary action taken against her alleged abuser because this was 'against the Data Protection Act'. This sounded unlikely so we asked the opinion of a legal expert and erstwhile District Judge. She laughed and told us in very robust language that the HR department was talking utter nonsense.

The administrator who oversees student complaints in a large university said that she had to work very hard to ensure that students who complained about the behaviour of other students were sent progress reports. After much cajoling, regular communication with the complainant was slowly becoming routine. However, complaints against staff are dealt with by the HR department and,

> "…they never seem to report back to anyone. It goes into HR and nothing ever seems to emerge."

Delays

Some of these communication problems would be less important if complaints of sexual abuse were dealt with quickly. Unfortunately the most common criticism we heard was that the procedures reached their conclusion far too slowly – often in months rather than weeks. One long-standing academic explained that the division of the academic year into three fairly short terms tends to slow down all university processes. Matters are often held over from one term to the next, and the break means that,

> "…an awful lot of recapping takes place before things move forward again."

This stop/start process might fit in well with academic work requiring reflection and further analysis but it can be desperately unfair on victim/survivors who have had to summon a great effort of will to make a report in the first place and want the whole thing brought to a conclusion as quickly as possible.

> "It seemed to go on forever. Every time I asked, I was told that it was all going to some committee or other. No one would tell me when it would end and I began to wish that I had not reported it in the first place."

Lengthy delays undermine the credibility of the system.

> "I don't see why they could not get together and sort it out straightaway. It made me think that I was not important enough."

Some of our interviewees thought that these long delays were the result of inefficiency.

> "Nothing seems to happen very quickly here."

But other people pointed out that lengthy delays operate to the university's benefit. Undergraduates stay for only a relatively short time and when they graduate, their complaint leaves with them. As one member of staff put it,

> "…the complaint just fades away."

A Student Union representative was equally suspicious. She had seen her university move very rapidly when managers were put under pressure.

> "Next to nothing happened for months but once the papers got hold of it, we had a result in a week."

One administrator told us that, if a complainant graduates and leaves the university before a decision is reached, the papers are destroyed and the complaint is expunged from the record. We have no way of knowing whether this is normal practice, but it might explain, for instance, the low level of complaints which were reported to the *Guardian* newspaper during its 2017 Freedom of Information inquiry.[9] When the results were published, the low numbers were greeted with derision by many students.

Perpetrators

Some victim/survivors were upset that universities seem to be so protective of the rights of students accused of sexual harassment and abuse. It was suggested that the events at Warwick University during 2018 and 2019 (and quoted in Chapter 2) 'prove' that the university's desire to allow the culprit to complete their studies is given greater importance than the need to provide justice to the victim/survivor.

However, deciding on an appropriate sanction for a student perpetrator can be difficult. One large university asked complainants how perpetrators should be punished. Predictably, this offered no solution.

> "In many cases the complainants did not really know what they wanted to happen to the perpetrators and, in some cases, the sanction they suggested was far too light to be appropriate."

This comment makes little sense until it is remembered that most sexual harassment and abuse is committed by someone whom the victim knows and, in many cases, knows well. They might even be in the same friendship group. As time passes and the initial horror fades, the accused often begins to get a measure of support from people who know them both. As one Student Union representative told us,

> "If he (the accused) gets a heavy penalty, his friends sometimes sympathise and the poor woman who suffered abuse is told she should not have got him into trouble. So she suffers twice."

Very often the complainant just wants the perpetrator to stop and be moved to a place where they are permanently out of her sight.

The general view of our interviewees is that perpetrators guilty of assault or of repeated incidents of abuse must be firmly punished. For other offences, a lesser penalty might be in order, providing – and this is a very important consideration – the victim/survivor is properly protected. There should be no repeat of incidents described elsewhere in this book where, for instance, restrictions on the perpetrator are relaxed and a victim/survivor faces the prospect of meeting or being in close proximity to their abuser.

As we explained in Chapter 2, we have been surprised that sexual abuse committed by staff is so common. We were also startled by the many allegations that universities do not pursue staff perpetrators with the vigour which we expected.

Many of the stories we were told followed a similar pattern. The victim is very much junior to the alleged perpetrator – sometimes a student and sometimes a junior academic. The abuse is denied or, if it cannot be denied, is minimised.

'She misunderstood. She should have known I was only joking.'

HR then carries out an investigation which the victim finds arduous and humiliating. If HR considers that the issue is serious enough, it goes to a disciplinary committee. A range of familiar defence arguments are deployed: the incidents did not happen, they have been exaggerated, the allegations are motivated by jealousy or spite, they were consensual or it only happened once, it was a momentary lapse and will never be repeated.

Although decisions are meant to be made on the balance of probability and should therefore be relatively easy to reach, meetings are frequently adjourned and the process often becomes lengthy. Rather than a clear cut outcome, the disciplinary committee will often settle for some 'compromise' which is accepted by the alleged perpetrator and avoids the committee having to apply a penalty. Some of the 'compromises' we heard about are

- The alleged perpetrator agrees not to communicate with the complainant.
- The alleged perpetrator agrees not to enter a particular building.
- The alleged perpetrator agrees not to go onto a particular floor (in the case we were told about, it was floor 3).
- The alleged perpetrator agrees to avoid entering campus by a particular route.

In several cases we were told that the outcome of the disciplinary process was not immediately announced but the alleged perpetrator just disappeared from campus. No one was officially told where the alleged perpetrator has gone.

> "We (the academics in the same department) had to cover his courses but, when we asked HR what had

happened, we were told that they did not know. A few weeks later we were told that he was not coming back. Eventually we discovered that his resignation had been accepted."

Sometimes there is a sequel. We know the names of three academics, who went through a disciplinary process, were found guilty and disappeared from campus only to reappear on the staff of another university.

This looks as if senior people are conspiring to help the perpetrator. Presumably the receiving university would have required a reference and presumably he (they are all male) would have been given a supportive reference even though he was found guilty of sexual abuse. Unless a credible alternative explanation is given, the suspicion will persist that the change in employment was agreed between the two universities so that a miscreant could be off-loaded in a manner which avoided publicity and legal risk. What the receiving university gets out of the deal is not clear but one member of staff, who had witnessed a tawdry example, guessed that the favour might be returned in the future.

This is a process which is well known in American universities. It even has a name. They call it:

'Pass the harasser'[10]

We asked whether staff in one of the receiving universities had been told about the harasser's background. They had not been told by the university, but once his appointment became common knowledge, two of the women whom he had abused sent messages to his new colleagues warning them to be very careful.

The effect of all this on the morale of staff at both universities is easy to imagine. All the universities which are involved say that they are committed to Zero Tolerance of sexual abuse. However, their behaviour in passing on a harasser in such a manner undermines this claim. One of the women who had been abused described the Zero Tolerance policy as

'a very sick joke'.

Protection

Most of the staff and students whom we interviewed believe that universities are very reluctant to penalise their senior staff even if the evidence against them is very strong.

"Mostly they just get away with it."

We asked why universities would want to give some employees special protection when any reluctance to discipline perpetrators is bound to damage the university's credibility. The answer we were given had three elements.

In the first place, we were told that established academics are protected by statutes designed to preserve freedom of expression and that their legal representative often uses these statutes in any disciplinary case where there is the possibility of dismissal.

Although put to us with conviction, this excuse did not seem credible. How on earth, we asked, can a person charged with sexual abuse possibly claim that their academic freedom is being infringed? We were told that it is sometimes argued that the complainant is a pawn in what is really an attack on the academic's ideas or publications. We continued to express scepticism but, after talking to several managers, we have had to accept that universities certainly strive to avoid dismissing established academics because it can involve a long legal case.

A second explanation offered by interviewees is even more worrying. Universities are keen to keep high-profile academics.

These are the people who enhance a university's reputation by developing new ideas, inventing new techniques and products, publishing extensively and perhaps even appearing from time to time in the media. One academic put it:

> "Universities love having star performers. They add a bit of gloss."

Another interviewee put it more personally:

> "Everyone likes to name-drop, including Vice Chancellors."

There are also practical advantages. Universities need their research to have 'impact', and an academic who can demonstrate interaction with decision-makers is highly prized. Well-known academics encourage more students to apply, and an increase in student numbers is the stated objective of many universities. Star performers attract money, in the form of research funding and sponsorship, a vital concern as budgets come under pressure.

All this is, of course, very desirable but the corollary, which many people described, is that star academics are being kept sweet by being given special treatment. This would not be a problem if the star performers behave impeccably. The trouble is that not all of them do. A sense of entitlement and a feeling of impunity is a dangerous combination. Some senior academics act as if they can set their own standards and expect others to accommodate what one junior academic described, with careful understatement, as their 'wiles and eccentricities'.

During our interviews we were told many awful stories of sexual abuse of students and junior academics by senior employees of the university. And we were told many worrying stories of the reluctance of universities to take firm action against perpetrators in senior academic positions, even when the case is strong. One woman explained what happens:

> "He keeps getting away with it because he is Head of (a) Department that is extremely successful and he is the recipient of several awards."

His name was one of several given to us. The allegations against all of them are known to the university authorities.

One academic wearily told us that this is not a new phenomenon. There are a host of stories of star academics from the past who could not keep their hands to themselves but escaped censure. One celebrated scholar even had a room named after him. Someone researched his career and found a large number of incidents of abusive behaviour. The reaction to this discovery was both surprising and revealing. Although a majority of academics wanted the room renamed, there was no shortage of voices arguing that the tribute to this brilliant but flawed scholar should remain.

> 'It all happened a long time ago when that sort of behaviour was more acceptable.'

And,

> '…we must not diminish respect for his scholarship.'

One famous scholar, who perhaps should have known better, expressed a

> '…certain wistful nostalgia', for the days when a female student might expect to be 'pawed about a bit' by her professor, when teaching had that 'erotic dimension' which had flourished after all since the time of Plato'.

These reactions suggest a third reason why a university might be tempted to avoid disciplining a senior academic. Too often a clutch of colleagues closes ranks around the perpetrator, making excuses, minimising the offence and stressing the miscreant's qualities as a scholar.

Many people have watched this piece of theatre at close quarters and disapproved of it profoundly.

> "I was amazed and upset that people who had condemned his behaviour when speaking to me, actually wrote to the Pro Vice Chancellor saying that he had done nothing wrong."

And in another university:

> "Lots of staff told the group of us who wanted him disciplined that they were on our side. But as soon as it became clear that the university was not going to take any action, the same people started offering him congratulations."

Sometimes the university gives away its reluctance to take action against a perpetrator by a careful redefinition of the offence,

> "What he had done was described as unfortunate when it should have been called reprehensible."

Staff Abuse of Students

Where a member of staff is accused of abuse against a student, the system is heavily weighted against the complainant.

Our research brought many surprises and perhaps the greatest was the revelation that almost every university permits their teaching staff to have sex with their students. We deal with this important issue in detail in Chapter 8. In this chapter we only consider the effect on the disciplinary process.

Because sex is allowed, a member of staff who is accused by a student of sexual abuse can claim that the sex act was consensual. We have been told of several incidents where the member of staff put pressure on the student by saying that he would tell everyone that she had agreed. Even when there are no threats, the student has to cope with the fear that making a report would badly disrupt her/his life at university. A first year student at a London university warns,

> 'It is ... difficult to speak out against a tutor if you're a student because you might potentially lose your advisor, your entire course – you might feel like you're putting your career in jeopardy.'[11]

With these pressures, it is understandable that well under one in ten of the students who say they have been sexually abused by a member of staff actually reported the incident.[12]

Those students who are brave enough to make a complaint face continuing difficulties. If the alleged assault is serious, the student is likely to be encouraged to go to the police. Few wish to do so because an interview by the police is frightening, a police inquiry is lengthy and the conviction rate is tiny.

On the other hand, if the university proceeds with the case as an internal matter, the member of staff is likely to be represented by an experienced trade union official while the student will only be accompanied by a friend or colleague from the Student Union, neither of whom will be familiar with the staff Disciplinary Procedure. This is no criticism of the trade union which has a responsibility to do the best for their member but, unless the university gives the student good advice and support, it will be an unequal struggle.

Human Resource Management

As we listened to the many criticisms of the current arrangements, we kept asking about the role of HR departments. If a university declares that it has a Zero Tolerance of sexual abuse, we believe it is for the HR department to recommend how that policy should be publicised and enforced. When a university wants an adequate reporting system, it is for the HR department to design a good system and to make sure it operates effectively. If the complaints and disciplinary systems are not working fairly, it is for the HR department to recommend and, if approved, carry through the required reforms. If it knows that a member of staff has a reputation for behaving in a sexually offensive manner towards students or staff, the HR department should investigate and, if necessary, recommend to the line manager that the alleged miscreant be warned about his/her behaviour.

These are important responsibilities, yet we heard of no HR department which was sufficiently active in this area of work. One academic who has campaigned for reform declared rather sadly that,

> "HR does not see the reduction of sexual abuse as one of its major functions."

HR Directors and their departments must take a share of the blame for the failure of universities to deal effectively with the problem of sexual abuse. The apparent reluctance of HR departments to take positive action has damaged the credibility of university policies.

Broken

What we heard from our many interviewees indicates that the system for dealing with sexual harassment and abuse in very many universities is broken. Of course it might be suggested that the many critical views which were expressed to us came from biased people and that the real situation is much better. There are convincing answers to that objection.

We were impressed by the apparent unanimity of much of the criticism. Not everyone agrees with every point, but there is considerable agreement on the fundamentals. Universities do not give a high priority to the problem of sexual harassment and abuse; they have not equipped themselves with the expertise and the specialist staff that are needed; many victim/survivors do not know how and to whom their complaints should be reported; universities are not very good at providing victim/survivors with the necessary advice and support; the way complaints are processed is complicated and often long-winded; communication with the victim/survivors during the investigations and any subsequent disciplinary action is usually poor; HR departments are too passive; concern for the perpetrator often appears to take priority over the needs of the victim/survivors; there is a strong suspicion that certain senior academics, in particular, believe that they can behave with an impunity, and this undermines the credibility in the whole system.

Of course, this catalogue of apparent failures is based on the expressed opinions of our interviewees. In the next two chapters we test their allegations by examining the evidence which is available. However, universities should be worried that their policies and practices are perceived so negatively. Perception is very important. It affects reputation; it conditions behaviour and has a strong influence on how people experience university life.

The truth, strongly expressed in our interviews, is that a significant part of the university community does not trust the current arrangements for handling the problem of sexual harassment and abuse. Many people have doubts about the good faith of the senior people who design and operate those arrangements. In short, a large number of people who study and work in higher education do not believe that universities are demonstrating an appropriate duty of care to their students and staff.

4

Evidence from the Media

The voices of the people we interviewed are powerful and unequivocal. Their testimony carries great conviction. Nevertheless we appreciate that, to the sceptic, whether in Higher Education or in Government, the stories they have told us and the opinions they have expressed might seem highly coloured and perhaps even partisan. So in this chapter and the next we move beyond perception and review the direct evidence which is available.

Sex Scandals

Since *The Telegraph* published its exposé of sexual harassment and abuse in 2014, the media have reported on many sex scandals in universities. The way universities have responded to this bad publicity follows a pattern which will be familiar to people who have received PR advice on how to close down a story. The universities admit to most of the details in the media report and accept that mistakes have been made. An apology is then issued and the university concerned gives an assurance that it will do better in future. This conciliatory reaction usually has the desired effect: there is little further for journalists to write and the media agenda moves on.

Taken together, the published scandals certainly look less like occasional aberrations and much more like the recurring symptoms of a systemic failure. To indicate their significance, we list the stories of sexual misconduct in universities which have been covered by the national media in the recent past. For completeness we include some scandals which we analyse elsewhere. The extent and nature of the list should correct any impression that our interviewees are exaggerating the severity of the problem.

- In January 2015 Hannah (not her real name), a student at **Exeter University,** says she was threatened with sexual violence twice in her first month at the university. On one occasion, a drunk student she did not know entered her room at 3a.m. and refused to leave (Hannah says this was a common 'joke' during Freshers' week, and guys would often rip the covers off sleeping female students). He told Hannah, 'I'm going to have sex with you, you're a slut'. He had to be physically removed by another male student.

    Hannah says that, on another occasion, the next-door student locked her in her room, turned off the lights and said, 'Bend over; I'm going to rape you'. Hannah was locked inside until other students heard her banging on the door and let her out. Hannah was scared, and her parents urged her to report it to the university. But the 18-year-old says she had no idea to whom she could speak, and did not trust university officials to do anything about it. (Telegraph)[1]

- In August 2015 Hannah Stubbs, a student at **Keele University** killed herself six months after reporting that she had been raped by another student. Her family claimed that the University had 'failed her'. (Independent).[2]

- In December 2015 a senior lecturer at **Sussex University** was charged with having assaulted the post graduate student with whom he was living. He was convicted of the offence in June 2016. The university did not suspend the senior lecturer until nine months after he was charged and only then after considerable criticism in the media. The Sussex University community was outraged. A letter was sent to the incoming Vice Chancellor signed by over 300 University of Sussex staff and students. The letter called for a public inquiry into the handling of the case, a task force to examine the University's policy and practice on issues of violence and harassment, and a commitment to the protection of all students in its care. An online petition signed by over 3,000 people called for the dismissal of the Senior Lecturer.

Faced with massive internal criticism, the incoming Vice Chancellor asked Professor Nicole Westmarland of Durham University to conduct a review. Her report was damning. She exposed many examples of poor practice and criticised the HR department for giving the wrong advice. She noted that the people she had interviewed felt that the student who was the victim had been,

> '...treated badly because of ... an apparent prioritisation of fairness to the member of staff and perpetrator.'[3]

Professor Westmarland was particularly critical of the risk assessment carried out by the university:

> 'The risk assessment was based solely on what the (Senior Lecturer) chose to tell the university with no external verification. No checks were made with the victim or student services... The academic undertaking the risk assessment did not have the knowledge, skills or experience required to conduct this risk assessment and the process was not documented.'[4]

After completing her report, Professor Westmarland was asked if Sussex was an isolated case. Her reply was unambiguous:

> 'It is the tip of the iceberg. Since being involved in the Sussex review I have had people from many other universities coming forward and telling me about their experiences and equally I've had other universities ask: was this just Sussex? And my answer is absolutely it isn't.'[5] (Independent).[6]

- In June 2016, Sara Ahmed, Director of the Centre for Feminist Research at **Goldsmiths, University of London,** resigned in protest at the alleged sexual harassment of students by staff. She said there had been six inquiries into four members of staff at the institution but there had been no public acknowledgment of the extent of the problem. Professor Ahmed wrote:

  > 'I have resigned in protest against the failure to address the problem of sexual harassment... When I talk about the problem of sexual harassment I am not talking about one rogue individual, or two, nor even a rogue unit, nor even a rogue institution. We are talking about how sexual harassment becomes normalised and generalised — as part of academic culture.' (Telegraph).[7]

- Allegations were also made to *The Times* during 2016 that students at **Goldsmiths** had become pregnant by academics and were later offered money in return for signing confidentiality agreements. A year later the Guardian revealed that Goldsmiths had paid out nearly £200,000 in compensation to students and staff. (Times and Guardian).[8]

- In January 2017 it was reported that 48% of female undergraduates at **Durham University** claimed to have been attacked. One said,

  'It's impossible to go on a night out here without being groped. Consent is a very blurred concept at Durham.'

  The report also included examples of the crude practices, designed to humiliate women, which we described in Chapter 2. (The Sun).[9]

- In January 2017 it was reported that Professor Andrew Dobson had resigned from his post at **Keele University** after it was discovered by police who raided his office that he had sexually explicit chats with underage girls and had downloaded images of child abuse on to his university computer. Dobson admitted that it was his 'fantasy' to have sex with girls under the age of 16. (Mirror).[10]

- In May 2017 **Bristol University** students who are part of the Revolt campaign group posted a Snapchat report of the experiences of 10 women who had been sexually harassed, assaulted or raped. All 10 women appeared on camera and told their story. Each of their faces was concealed to protect their identity. One said:

  'In my first term of freshers I walked a drunk friend home after a night out. I refused to let anything happen but he said, "It's not rape - you want this."'[11] (Daily Mail).[12]

- In October 2017 **Cambridge University** made the widely-welcomed decision to record anonymous reports of sexual harassment and abuse. An increase in reports was expected but, when the university reported that it had received 173 reports in three months, the size of the surge surprised many people in the university. (Guardian).[13]

The response of Graham Virgo, Pro Vice Chancellor for Education at the University of Cambridge, was more measured. He wrote in a blog:

> 'It supports our belief that we have a significant problem involving sexual misconduct – what we now need to ensure is that those who have been affected receive the support and guidance they need.'

When **Oxford University** started recording anonymous complaints, it also found that the number of reports of sexual harassment and abuse increased fivefold.

- In June 2018 media stories began to appear about an internet network set up by male students at **Warwick University,** in which the students exchanged messages about how they would like to sexually assault and rape women in the university. As we recorded in Chapter 2, one woman known to the men was named and one of the internet messages suggested that the men should,

  > 'Rape her in the street while everybody watches.'

  When the so-called 'rapechat' was reported, the university accepted that the allegations were 'extremely serious', ordered an investigation and held a disciplinary panel. One student was suspended for life, two for 10 years and two for one year. The two students suspended for 10 years subsequently appealed and their suspension was reduced to one year. After a long delay this appeal decision was revealed and caused distress to the women named, who were frightened that they would meet the offenders again on campus. Demonstrations took place in support of the women and soon afterwards the Vice Chancellor stated that, in spite of the appeal decision, the male students would not return to the university. Many aspects of the university's behaviour have been severely criticised, including the decision to use its apparently untrained Director of Press and Media Relations as the investigating officer and the conflict of interest which arose from this appointment. The Vice Chancellor ordered an enquiry. (The Times and most other newspapers).[14]

- In July 2018 Dr Emma Chapman accused **UCL** of trying to silence her after she had made a complaint of harassment against a staff member. Nearly two years passed and her complaint had not been dealt with. During this time the university tried to persuade her to sign a non-disclosure agreement (NDA) preventing her from speaking about her complaint. She eventually reached a settlement of £70,000 and won a legal waiver allowing her to describe what had happened to her. The press report states that,

  > '…the staff member accused of harassment denied many of Dr Chapman's claims and was allowed to continue working at UCL after an investigation concluded.' (Evening Standard).[15]

- In May 2019, it was revealed that **Essex University**, although committed to dealing with sexual abuse cases within 60 days, had allowed many complaints to be outstanding for very much longer. 38 students have reported sexual harassment under a new system which was introduced in 2018. Many students have protested that there is a large backlog and many delays. One student said that although she had reported a serious sexual assault 10 months earlier, a hearing date had only just been set.

  > 'It's made me feel like I have been taken advantage of not just by him, but by the university. I feel they silenced it. He is still able to walk around on campus… and nothing has been done about it. It doesn't give me any closure.' (BBC).[16]

- In June 2019, geography student Karli Wagener, 20 claimed she was choked and raped by a fellow undergraduate. She waived her right to anonymity so she could criticise her university's handling of the case. She said that **Leicester University** had failed to protect her by allowing her alleged attacker to remain at the university while she was put on a three-month waiting list for counselling. She says she suffered PTSD and panic attacks as a result of bumping into her alleged attacker on campus. Police are investigating the attack. (The Times).[17]

- During August 2019 A **Cambridge University** student claimed that her case of sexual assault had been dropped following a ruling by Cambridge's discipline committee that sexual misconduct should no longer be covered by the university's general disciplinary regulations. She had made a complaint of rape against a male student and said that the change was denying her justice. She said that Cambridge University's decision has turned her, 'from a survivor to a victim'.

  > 'I wasn't fighting to get justice for what happened to me any more – I was powerless.'

  Cambridge academics and Student Union officials condemned the university's response to the ruling, which they said had left vulnerable women without any internal means to pursue complaints of sexual assault and rape. (Guardian).[18]

- In September 2019 the BBC's *File on 4* programme claimed that there are,

  > '...serious flaws in the way many universities mismanage (sic) reports of sexual assaults and harassment'. It went on to state that, 'some students believe they're re-victimised and bullied into keeping their complaints quiet.'

Students told the BBC reporter that they believe universities are more interested in protecting their reputations than their students and serial offenders are still at large.

> 'Even when perpetrators are dealt with, they're often given derisory sentences.' (BBC).[19]

- In October 2019 the BBC published the results of a Freedom of Information request, which showed that reports of rape, sexual assault and harassment made to UK universities had trebled in three years. They recorded 1,436 allegations of sexual harassment or sexual violence against students in 2018-19 - up from 476 in 2016-17. The data, from 124 of 157 universities, shows not all universities have robust systems to prevent or respond to sexual violence.

  The BBC added that the increase may partially reflect the fact that some universities have made it easier for students to report allegations and receive support - three years ago universities promised action amid concern about sexual violence on campus. Universities said they are making progress in dealing with the issue. (BBC).[20]

- In October 2019 Trinity Hall, Cambridge, revealed that they were allowing an academic, Dr Peter Hutchinson, to return to the College less than two years after being permanently excluded. Hutchinson's exclusion had followed a formal complaint by 10 students who gave details of 'inappropriate, sexual and sexist comments' which he had allegedly made. At that time, in 2015, he had been allowed to stay in the college after allegedly accepting a ban preventing him from contacting undergraduates. When it was claimed in 2017 that he had breached this ban, the college's Senior Tutor, Dr Clare Jackson, said that he,

'...will not be present in college at any time in the future.'

As soon as it became known that Hutchinson would once again be able to attend college events, there were protests by Cambridge academics and students. One of the students who made a complaint about Hutchinson in 2015 said,

> 'I am incredibly disheartened that, yet again, after a four year process to get him removed, the forces of power and patronage win out over empty commitments to zero tolerance and support and safety for students of the college.'

After a letter was signed by about 1,400 current and past members of the College, Hutchinson announced that he was resigning. Trinity Hall will now be carrying out a review of its procedures. (Guardian).[21]

A few months later it was revealed that in 2015 Hutchinson had self published a 'sexually charged' novel using a pseudonym about academics watching students having sex. (Observer).[22]

- In November 2019, Birmingham University refused to investigate a report by a student that she had been raped by another student because the alleged incident took place off campus in privately rented student accommodation. The university said it could not deal with allegations of misconduct which did not take place,

  > '...during a university related activity or on university premises.'

  The University also cited the long delay in reporting the alleged rape as a second reason for its refusal to investigate. The alleged victim was very upset. She said that,

  > 'It didn't feel like the university believed me.'

UUK criticised the university's decision saying that universities should investigate rape complaints whether the incident was alleged to have occurred on campus or not. (Guardian)[23]

- In February 2020 Dr Jeremy the Master of **Trinity Hall, Cambridge University**, agreed to "step back" from his duties following allegations that he had he mishandled students' complaints about sexual misconduct. At the same time Dr William O'Reilly, a Trinity Hall staff fellow, has also stepped back from teaching and supervision work after being criticised for his role in overseeing the disciplinary process triggered by three women who had made allegations of rape and sexual assault against a male student in 2018. (Telegraph).[24]

- Also in February 2020, more than more than 600 students signed a letter raising concerns over how sexual misconduct allegations are dealt with at **Cambridge University**. (Telegraph).[25]

- In March 2020, in the course of a long running dispute about the behaviour of the Very Reverend Dr Martyn Percy, Dean of **Christ Church, Oxford University**, it was reported that Dr Percy had heard an allegation that a former student had been sexually assaulted during their time at Christ Church, whilst still a minor. Upon further investigation, it is apparent that this allegation was disclosed to the Dean, but never reported by him to the police, the local authority designated officer, Christ Church's safeguarding officers, or the Church of England's safeguarding officer.' (Church Times).[26]

- In April 2020, the **University of Derby** suspended six male students over "degrading and offensive" comments allegedly made about their peers in an online group chat. The men are accused of being part of a group which exchanged crude sexual remarks, including a rape joke, about several female students. The university has launched an investigation into the conduct of the students, five of whom are on a policing course and the sixth is studying business.

The University took action after screenshots were posted online that allegedly showed details of a group chat in which the men rated the appearances of female students, and one of them joked about using child rape in a chat-up line. The screenshots of the alleged group chat that were shared online were described by another student as 'disgusting and misogynistic'. Two of the students alleged to have been part of the group chat are special constables with Derbyshire Constabulary, and have been suspended while the force investigates their conduct.

A University of Derby spokeswoman said:

> 'We were incredibly disappointed to see the degrading and offensive language used in online forums about some of our female students. Such behaviour is unacceptable, will not be tolerated and is being addressed with the utmost urgency. The male students involved in making these comments have been suspended and we are working with an external specialist agency to carry out a full and formal investigation.' (Guardian).[27]

A study of these media reports shows that two significant changes have occurred during the last three years. The first is more obvious. The number of media stories has steadily increased so that, towards the end of the period, a new story has broken every month. This is in spite of the fact that for some of the time the media agenda was almost entirely focused on the coronavirus pandemic. It is not clear whether this change indicates an increase in sexual misconduct in universities or whether it shows a greater media interest in finding and reporting such stories. Whichever explanation is correct, there is no doubt that media pressure on universities is intensifying.

The second change is in the nature of the media reports. We noted in Chapter 1 that an important reason why universities have been able to contain and even neutralise media pressure was because, until about 2015, journalists tended to regard every story of sexual harassment and abuse as an isolated case. They usually accepted assurances by universities that these 'exceptions' took place against a background of good governance by universities. That has now changed and media reports are increasingly suggesting that there is a general problem of sexual harassment and abuse which universities are not handling very well. If this trend continues, and we believe that the media's new approach is supported by the facts, explanations given by universities are likely to be subjected to much more rigorous scrutiny. We welcome this change, but it is likely to cause significant problems for individual universities and for UUK.

Lessons

If universities review these media reports they will find that there are many lessons to be learnt.

First of all, universities should accept the evidence from both Cambridge and Oxford that sexual harassment and abuse are much more pervasive than most institutions have assumed. The decision by Oxford and Cambridge to record anonymous complaints has resulted in a large increase in the number of reported incidents.

The gradual acceptance of anonymous reporting by more universities probably explains why, in 2019, the BBC found that the number of reported allegations of sexual harassment or violence had more than trebled in three years.[28] However, surveys of victim/survivors which have taken place during this period indicate that, even when anonymous reporting is allowed, the proportion of victims who inform the university of their ordeal is still depressingly low. Universities should take notice of the research on underreporting and realise that, even with anonymous reporting, they would still have to multiply the number of reports of harassment and assaults by a factor of 10 to get close to an accurate figure. Where anonymous reporting is not allowed, universities should appreciate that they may only be hearing about 1 in 20 of the incidents which occur.

Therefore the first lesson is to take a realistic view of the extent of the problem. If universities had appreciated how many students and staff were being harassed and abused and had devoted an appropriate level of resource to remedial action, many of the scandals reported by the media would probably not have taken place.

Other failures which are highlighted in the media reports should be addressed. Young women do not always have adequate protection in the first months of their university career; early and effective support to students and staff who suffer sexual harassment and abuse is still not universally available; there is the need to deal more decisively with what, in Chapter 2 we called 'lad culture'; students and staff are not being properly shielded from sexual predators in senior positions. Finally, there is the essential requirement to have regulations and procedures in place which work effectively and in a timely fashion without the need for trickery or discreditable cover-ups.

In our interviews we heard many allegations that university managers are not applying their established rules and procedures in a fair-minded manner. But there were also strong complaints that the procedures themselves are defective. It was alleged that the procedures are hidden from view, difficult to understand and have not been modernised to reflect the change in public expectations which has followed the revelations of extensive sexual abuse in the entertainment industries and elsewhere.

The media reports tend to support the claims of the people we interviewed. Under pressure, the procedures operated by five universities and one university college failed miserably. Is this evidence of a more general malaise? We decided to delve more deeply and that investigation is the subject of the next chapter.

5

A Failing Process

The scandals recorded in the media demonstrate beyond doubt that many universities are not good at handling either incidents or complaints of sexual harassment and abuse. But it is not clear whether these problems are confined to those universities which have suffered the scandals or whether there is a more general problem. And do the problems result from human error by the managers and administrators who deal with the cases or is there a deeper explanation? Are the policies and procedures operated by universities fit for purpose?

We decided that the only way we could answer these important questions was to examine the regulations, procedures and ordinances which universities use when dealing with sexual harassment and abuse. And since we wanted to discover the full extent of any problem, we decided that looking at a few universities was not good enough. We had to examine them all.

The Freedom of Information Requests

We sent a Freedom of Information (FOI) request to every university in England and Wales, asking them to send us copies of the procedures which they use when a complaint is made of sexual harassment or sexual abuse. Details of the FOI request is attached as an appendix at the end of this chapter.

A total 102 universities were contacted.[1] Although there were inevitably a number of hiccups and glitches, we were given a good deal of cooperation and eventually we received a return from every university.

The task of analysis was formidable. A total 738 documents were either sent to us or drawn to our attention, and most of them are lengthy. It took many weeks to read them all and to record their particular characteristics. What we found was fascinating: by turns reassuring and dispiriting.

We accept, of course, that the procedures, although extensive and detailed, cannot tell the whole story. A bad procedure can be implemented with understanding and sympathy, just as a good procedure can be applied brusquely and without compassion. Nevertheless the nature and the wording of the procedures provide powerful evidence about how universities regard sexual harassment and abuse and how they think people who claim to be victims and people accused of being perpetrators should be treated.

In the past few years, Britain has been forced to abandon the indulgent attitude to sexual abuse which had been so common in the 1980s and 1990s. The naming of Savile, Harris, Hall, Clifford and other celebrities as serial abusers and the testimony of their victims have demonstrated that sexual abuse is not something to be dismissed with a wink or a joke. There is a growing realisation that sexual abuse can have a devastating effect on the victim, leaving a residue of fear, distress, guilt and shame which can last for decades.

Many organisations have responded to these welcome changes in public attitudes by giving a higher priority to reducing sexual harassment and abuse. Companies, charities, public bodies and even some political parties[2] have developed better methods of supporting victims and ensuring that complaints are dealt with sympathetically and expeditiously. To assist them, the Advisory

Conciliation and Arbitration Service (ACAS) has issued useful guidelines which we described in Chapter 1. The current situation is far from ideal, but significant progress has been made.

We started our analysis by looking to see whether similar improvements have been made by universities in England and Wales. Have they developed a more modern and enlightened approach, have they carried through significant reforms or have they been content to rely on long-standing procedures and practices?

Overview

We discovered that universities have responded to the change in public attitudes in very different ways. At one end of the scale are those institutions which are undertaking a major review of their methods and procedures. Typically their determination to change is stated by their Vice Chancellors in high-profile statements on their website and sometimes in interviews and conference speeches.

At the other end of the scale is a much larger group of universities which, judging by the contents of their procedures, appear to have done very little to reform and improve. Most of the documents we examined show a date when they were last reviewed. We got used to seeing dates which indicated that no change had been made for 10 or, in a few cases, nearly 20 years. We also found a slew of grammatical mistakes and typos – a clear indication that some of these documents are not being consulted very often.

Every university is different but, to sum up what we found, we place universities in three categories:

- The worst performers might be said to be traditionalist in their approach. These universities appear to have made few changes in the recent past and show no obvious sign of giving a high priority to sexual harassment and abuse. Moreover, there is little indication that much expert advice or support is readily available to victims and survivors within the university.

Almost a third of Universities (32) Are in This Category.

- The largest group of universities is made up of what might be called cautious reformers. These universities have typically introduced some new initiatives to address sexual harassment and abuse. Reporting methods have often been improved, systems of advice and support have usually been strengthened and the issue has been given a higher priority on their website and in their publications. Many of these universities have also worked closely with their Student Union and sometimes with the trade unions in developing campaigns which publicise good practice and condemn unacceptable behaviour.

These developments are to be applauded but unfortunately the reforms have generally left much of the traditional system unchanged. Old procedures remain in place and, to a great extent, determine how complaints of sexual harassment and abuse are dealt with. As we demonstrate later, these long-established procedures are both difficult to understand and are unsuitable for use in cases of sexual harassment or abuse.

About 60% of universities (61) are amongst this group of cautious reformers.

- Regrettably we found only a small number of universities who seem prepared to make the fundamental changes in policy and procedures which are necessary to deal effectively with sexual harassment and abuse. These universities are decisive in their commitment to reform.

So far, no university has completed the process and there are problems still to be overcome. Developing new procedures requires a great deal of consultation and committee management. We also believe that every one of these universities is under-funding their new programme of reform.

However, what distinguishes this small group of universities is a willingness to adopt a more professional and evidence-based approach. They have appointed specialists, collected better quality information and set about developing policies and procedures which are specifically designed to deal with the very particular problem of sexual harassment and abuse.

We found only 9 universities which appear to be heavily committed to making the substantial changes which we believe are necessary.

They are:

> University of Cambridge, University of Durham, Goldsmiths University of London, Imperial College London, Keele University, Lancaster University, London School of Economics, University of Oxford and University of Sussex.

Anyone who knows the university sector will be surprised by some of the names on this list. In the last chapter we described the sex scandals which the media have reported in the recent past. Five of these nine progressively minded universities were involved in those damaging reports, and we have already noted that two of them got into serious difficulties specifically because of failures in the operation of their procedures.

We questioned a number of insiders, and it was suggested to us that the damaging publicity acted as a wake-up call to those universities which were targets of media criticism. Direct experience of the damage caused by the failure to address the problem of sexual harassment and abuse in a professional manner evidently convinced them that fundamental reform was necessary. If this suggestion is correct, then we are glad that something worthwhile has come out of all the misery and suffering.

Our Viewpoint

We examined key aspects of the university procedures to determine how they would appear to a person reporting sexual harassment or abuse. We adopted this viewpoint because, as we described in Chapter 2, sexual harassment and abuse causes great distress to the victims. We believe that, above all else, the procedures should provide a sympathetic pathway for victim/survivors to achieve justice.

Of course, other considerations are important. The procedures should help to deter potential perpetrators. People should be protected from unfounded accusations. And because universities must be a force for good in our society, they should be seen to be acting in a reasonable, fair-minded and humane manner. However, in our view, achieving these objectives is worth little unless universities are seen to be fair to the victims/survivors. The procedures should aim to ensure that, whenever a member of the university community suffers sexual harassment or abuse, they will receive the consideration and justice that their university owes, as a duty of care, to its students and staff.

We were confirmed in our opinion by a discussion with Vera Baird, the Victims Commissioner. She talked to us about the need for 'procedural justice'. While the outcome of a court case is obviously important, the victim is deeply affected by the way s/he is treated during the proceedings. Vera Baird said that too often victims are ignored or marginalised; this experience can be very damaging and often increases the victim's distress. Victims need to feel that they are given proper attention from beginning to end.

For this reason, the first question in our minds when we examined the details of the procedures, has been,

- Does this clause or this practice demonstrate a high level of concern for the victim/survivor?

Access to Advice

People who have been harassed or abused are likely to be upset, confused and vulnerable. They need rapid access to good advice. So the first question must be: where do they get it? Every university says that the answer is to be found on their university website. To test this encouraging belief we put ourselves in the position of a victim/survivor seeking help. We selected 10 university websites at random and searched on the words,

> *Sexual abuse, sexual assault, sexual harassment, and rape.*

The results differed considerably. The good news is that, when the search was made, 3 of the 10 university websites immediately highlighted the university's support for students and staff who had suffered sexual harassment or abuse, offering practical advice and support. Another university provided accessible information which was almost as good.

However, when we put these key words into the search facility of five other websites, what came up was not guidance and help for victims but a list of research work being carried out on sexual matters by academics in the university. Top of one screen was the biography of an academic. Top of the screen on another website was a description of a report 'Measuring the scale and changing nature of child sexual abuse and child sexual exploitation.'

With persistence, we eventually found details of each university's advice and support policies. This vital information is always listed but is often buried on the second or third page. No one can reasonably claim that these websites are meeting the needs of a distressed victim who is looking for instant assistance.

Our experience with the 10th website was worse. It was almost impossible to access because a large panel warning of cookies kept reappearing however often the 'I accept' button was pressed.

The best of the 10 random websites which we chose was that operated by Keele University. A search on any of the key words produces a well-presented screen entitled 'Sexual Violence', displaying a telephone number and email address to contact, if (as the website puts it), 'you or someone else is in danger'.

This is followed by a series of icons showing what to do next and how to get advice and support. Then there is a photograph of the members of Keele University's Sexual Violence Prevention and Support Team with an invitation to call their dedicated telephone number.

After comparing these results we wondered why, when some universities adopt such a straightforward and helpful approach, other universities are not doing the same.

Reporting an Incident

For all the compelling reasons we have explained in Chapter 2, victims find it very difficult to report sexual harassment and abuse. So universities should make reporting as easy as possible.

If a university has a sexual violence team made up of properly trained specialists, the process can be straightforward. The potential complainant is directed to that team and support and advice is available from expert personnel. Sometimes the names of team members are given and that makes it easier for the victim to contact the specialist team and to begin that difficult first conversation.

All this seems very professional and reassuring. Unfortunately, the bad news is that we can find only 17 universities which have a trained sexual violence team led by a specialist. Other universities – more than 80% of the sector – use different and, in our opinion, inferior reporting processes.

In the group of universities which lack trained specialists, the potential complainant is usually directed to a department, often Student Services for students and HR for staff. However, complainants are rarely told whom to ask for. Some universities have designated a group of staff as Harassment or Dignity Advisors and recommend that victims contact those individuals. But most of these Advisors are volunteers with other jobs to do, and their availability cannot be guaranteed.

Some universities appear to believe that it is helpful to list a large number of people and departments who are tasked with receiving complaints. Two universities have a list of eight possible places to report and over 30 have four, five or six. The trouble with this approach is that it is very unlikely that such a large number of people will be properly trained and experienced. Course tutors, who are often listed, will no doubt try to comfort a student who is upset but they are unlikely to be able to do much more than pass the student onto Student Services.

Many universities also suggest that, at night and weekends, victims should contact the university security service. We saw no indication in the documents that security officers are properly trained to give adequate support to victims who will be fearful and vulnerable. This may be a gap in the paperwork because Professor Julia Buckingham told us that Brunel University is very careful in training its security staff to give support to victims of sexual harassment and abuse. They are experienced in handling distressed people and are trained by the Metropolitan Police. Other universities may do something similar but there must be a residual problem because we heard so many stories from our interviewees of security staff behaving in a dismissive or offhand manner to students in trouble.

Overall, our strong impression is that, outside the relatively small group of universities which employ well-trained teams led by a specialist and a few others which have made special arrangements, the reporting system has not received enough attention. Too often it seems somewhat hit and miss.

Restrictions

These reporting problems are compounded by the restrictions which many universities apply. Most universities will not receive a complaint unless the complainant gives their name. Even one of the nine most progressive universities states in its procedures that it will only take note of a report if it is given enough information to allow investigation. Another university has a well-constructed reporting process but is adamant on this point. Its student complaints procedure includes the bald statement:

> 'Anonymous complaints will not be investigated.'[3]

This approach is understandable but short-sighted. For all the reasons given in Chapter 2, victims are reluctant to report and, when they do report, are reluctant to give their name. So universities which refuse to accept anonymous reporting only learn about a small minority of sexual harassment and abuse incidents. Allowing anonymous reporting would give them a much better idea of the number of incidents which actually occur. Anonymous reporting might also provide other intelligence. If the same name keeps cropping up in the anonymous reports as an alleged abuser, it might be worth asking that person about his/her behaviour.

More fundamentally, a refusal to take account of anonymous complaints tends to undermine the credibility of the reporting system. If a victim or a well-motivated observer is turned away because they will not give their name, they are unlikely to believe that the university is doing everything possible to combat sexual harassment and abuse.

These are strong arguments and we hope that the tide is turning. The *Report and Support* initiative which has been adopted by several of the universities which we have called cautious reformers, includes the facility to record anonymous complaints. Naturally this change is only effective if the whole university community is properly informed. We quoted an example in Chapter 3 when this had unfortunately not been done.

The second restriction concerns the timing of the incident which prompted the complaint. Many universities will only investigate complaints if the incident occurred recently. Some require complaints to be made within three weeks of the incident, another group specify a month and a large number of universities require complaints to be submitted within three months of the date of the incident occurred.

We appreciate that a time limit for complaints about such routine matters as the quality of accommodation or access to IT might be justifiable but setting a time limit for the submission of complaints of sexual harassment and abuse takes no account of the mental state of the victim. Many victim/survivors told us that the decision about whether or not to report an incident was very difficult. Sexual harassment and abuse leaves the victim with a heavy burden of fear, shame and guilt. The temptation to do nothing which will prolong the agony is very strong. 40% of victims told an NUS survey that they did not tell anyone – not friends, not family, not the university and not the police.[4] Several of the victim/survivors we interviewed told us that we were the first people to hear their story.

Victim/survivors need time to come to terms with what has happened. Eventually some, who were initially reluctant, might change their mind and be prepared to report. But this might take weeks, months or, in some cases, even longer. Placing some arbitrary time limit on what can be reported means that, once again, the Vice Chancellor and senior managers will have a very imperfect view of what is going on in their university. More important, a time limit on reporting deprives many victim/survivors of the opportunity to secure the justice they deserve.

We accept that historic cases are difficult to investigate. Nevertheless universities which profess a zero tolerance of sexual harassment and abuse have an obligation to do as much as possible. At the very least they can keep a record of the submission, check whether the name of the alleged perpetrator has been reported before and examine whether the circumstance of the alleged incident points to the need for a change in security measures.

Fortunately some university procedures contain clauses which allow the university to follow up a complaint which is out of time, providing it is sufficiently serious. These clauses are useful but we maintain that the case for removing all time limits is compelling. Victim/survivors ought not to face the added burden of trying to prove their case is serious enough to be considered after the deadline has been passed. Victim/survivors need time to come to terms with their awful experiences, and their universities should show enough goodwill and sympathy to allow them that time.

Understanding

Once a person makes a complaint, s/he naturally wants to know how it will be handled. Unfortunately the procedure for handling complaints of sexual harassment or abuse is rarely set out in a single document. Every university has a batch of procedures which interlock and sometimes overlap. Students are typically covered by a Student Conduct policy and procedure, a Complaints procedure, a Disciplinary procedure, a Dignity at Study procedure and often by an Anti-Harassment and Bullying procedure. Members of staff are typically covered by a Grievance procedure, a Disciplinary procedure, a Dignity at Work procedure and perhaps by an Anti-Harassment and Bullying procedure. In addition there are Equality and Diversity Policies, sometimes with attached procedures.

This is a mountain of information and making sense of it all would challenge the concentration of the most diligent lawyer. As we know from our interviews, it can totally demoralise a person whose emotions are already raw in the aftermath of sexual abuse.

Unfortunately it is not even obvious which procedure will be used to handle each complaint. At first sight it might be assumed that a student making a complaint of sexual abuse against another student would use the Student Complaints procedure but we were told by some universities that is not the case. Often they would use the Anti-Bullying and Harassment procedure. However, a complaint by a student against a member of staff would normally be made using the Student Complaints procedure. It is all very confusing.

Even if the route which the university intends to follow is explained to the complainant, the process is not straightforward. None of these procedures stand alone. It is very common for the chosen procedure to contain a phrase which states,

> 'This procedure should be read in conjunction with... ', followed by a list of other procedures which must be taken into account.

Usually between three and six procedures are listed but one university refers to 18 separate procedural documents which should be considered.

There are few shortcuts. If the complainant wants to understand the process, s/he will have to read all the documents which are listed. This is a daunting task. The language is off-putting with many legal phrases, complex clauses and a great deal of cross-referencing. The documents are long: the procedural documents are rarely shorter than 10 pages and some are double that length. A few universities have added flowcharts to show how these complex procedures might be navigated. Many flowcharts are useful, but some simply confirm the complexity of the process. In one flowchart we found that a single box contained 280 words.

Perhaps with the best of intentions, some of those universities which might be described as cautious reformers have created further confusion by adding the policy called *Report and Support* to the existing procedures. The laudable aim is to strengthen the universities' commitment to zero tolerance by encouraging victims to report and by assuring them that they will supported.

Unfortunately this modern-looking statement does not usually replace the long-established procedures about complaints, grievances and discipline but adds a new layer of policy and procedural complexity. Because the old procedures have not been replaced, their requirements have to be met. Therefore, at some stage in the process, the complainant finds that the university will leave behind the bright modernity of *Report and Support* and revert to the traditional procedures with all the obscure phrases, complicated clauses and legalese.

That takes us to the core problem. The university procedures have certainly not been written to be easily understood by a complainant. Very little account is taken of the mental state of a victim who will be trying to recover from a debilitating experience and needs to receive information which is straightforward and reassuring. The tone should be sympathetic. After all, the complainant is complying with the university's request to report abuse and has very little to gain from making a report. Indeed, the complainant might well become a target of abuse on social media once the allegation becomes public knowledge. So s/he is entitled to strong support from the university. Yet it is rare for the documents to offer a word of thanks or gratitude. Most are not even written in a manner which recognises her/his ordeal and the strain that making a report will entail.

Instead, the procedures read as if their main purpose is to provide the university with strong legal protection against any claim which might be made against the institution. Perhaps this is a hangover from the Zellick Principles which were described in Chapter 1 or perhaps it is just that lawyers, acting in what they regard as the university's best interest, have played too dominant a part in shaping the documents.

Nevertheless, whatever the motives of those writing the procedures, there can be no doubt that the procedures are complicated and difficult to understand. Because they overlap and interlock, even a complainant who studies them closely cannot be sure how the procedures will operate in her/his particular case. Instead of clarity, certainty and warmth there is complexity, confusion and a coldness which implies that the complainant has done something to be ashamed of.

A Similar Path

We went on to examine how a complaint of sexual harassment and abuse would be handled in practice and whether the process is fair and appropriate. Our task was made easier because of a helpful discovery. Although the wording of the procedures is complex and the details vary, the main procedures follow a similar pattern.

This mainstream approach involves taking complaints, by students or members of staff, through the following stages:

1. First there is an *informal* process.
2. Second is the *formal* stage when a complaint can be lodged.
3. This is followed by an *investigation* by a university manager or official.
4. A *report of the investigator's findings* goes to a senior executive of the university, who decides whether, at first sight, the complaint is justified.
5. If so, *disciplinary action* will be taken against the person who is the subject of the complaint.
6. That person's guilt or innocence will be determined according to the rules of the university's *disciplinary policy*.
7. If that person disagrees with the verdict, they have the *right of appeal* to an appeal panel.

This is an onerous process and problems occur right at the start. Complainants usually feel that as soon as they have told a university official, their complaint has been lodged and the university will take action. That is not what happens. By and large, universities will not follow the matter up within the procedure until a *formal* complaint is made at the second stage.

The complainant reaches this second stage by passing through the *informal* stage. We were amazed by what we found there.

Incredible as it will appear, the *informal* stage often encourages the complainant to approach the person against whom their complaint has been made, and attempt to reach an informal agreement with them. For the avoidance of doubt, the university is actually asking a victim of sexual abuse to contact the perpetrator, who is probably the last person in the world they wish to see, and try to reach some sort of agreement. No wonder victims are aghast when this is explained to them. It is difficult to think of a more inappropriate and frightening proposal to make to a victim of sexual abuse.

The procedures go into detail. The relevant clauses usually include a sentence which considers the possibility that the alleged victim might not wish to approach the alleged perpetrator on their own. In these circumstances, the procedure suggests that the alleged victim might be accompanied. One university even mentions assertiveness training for people who find this process difficult. Alternatively the procedure suggests that the complainant might prefer someone else to meet the alleged perpetrator on the complainant's behalf. Most procedures also offer the complainant a process of mediation by which a third party would help the alleged victim and the alleged perpetrator to resolve the complaint.

Of course a university can say in explanation that the complainant is not required to accept any of the possibilities listed at the *informal* stage and this is true. But since none of these possibilities is appropriate in a case of sexual harassment and abuse, we wonder why on earth they are included in the procedure. Their effect is to make a victim feel frightened, vulnerable and unsupported.

And anyone who suggests that the informal stage can be entirely ignored should re-read the procedures. Almost every document makes it clear that the informal stage must be passed through before a formal complaint can be submitted. As one university typically explains:

> 'No formal complaint will be accepted unless the matter has been considered at the informal stage.'

The Right to Know

Unfortunately this apparent lack of concern for the feelings of the complainant runs through most of the complaints process.

The *investigation* by a university nominated employee, usually a senior manager, obviously has a crucial effect on the outcome. The complainant will want to explain her/his complaint to the investigator. This usually happens as a matter of necessity – the investigator needs to hear the details of the complaint – but the nature and length of the interview, the provision of adequate time for the complainant to prepare and the right of the complainant to return for a second meeting once the investigator has seen the accused is not guaranteed in most of the procedures.

Once the *investigation* is completed, the complainant will want to know whether disciplinary action is to be taken against the person s/he has accused. We can find only a few procedures which guarantee that the complainant will be given this information. Indeed the procedures typically give the complainant no right to receive progress reports on what is happening throughout the complaints process.

The most serious failure is the absence, in most procedures, of any commitment to inform the complainant of the outcome of the case. Some are sensible and straightforward: the best give an unequivocal guarantee that the complainant will be told of the outcome at exactly the same time as the accused. But a majority of the procedures include no such assurance. Almost all of the staff procedures are silent on this point.

Some universities seem to believe that they are prohibited by Data Protection legislation from telling the complainant the outcome of their complaint. This is completely false, and we trust that correct advice will be given to all universities in the near future. This is not some procedural nicety. Complainants are entitled to know whether their complaints have been accepted and, if the accused remains on campus, what measures they need to take to protect themselves, both physically and mentally.

Completion

Complainants naturally want their cases to be settled as soon as possible. Many have struggled to find the strength to make a complaint in the first place and they want an early decision so that they can try to put the horrible experience behind them and get back to some normality. We were disappointed to find that in this respect, as in many others, the complainant's peace of mind is given much less importance than it deserves.

Many of the procedures which we have examined do not specify any time limit for the case to be completed. A few say that it is very difficult to specify a completion date because all complaints are different. Many more commit themselves to act 'promptly' or state that they will 'strive to avoid delay.' A favourite phrase is, 'as soon as possible'.

The minority of universities which commit themselves to a completion date range from an impressive 20 days at Anglia Ruskin University to three months at a number of other universities. Three months seems a long time but even a date as distant as this gives the complainant some security. Without a completion date and without the guarantee of regular updates the complainant has to keep asking what is happening to her/his case.

The impression we gained from reading the procedures was that once the investigation is over, the complainant's role is regarded as at an end and the focus moves to the accused and to the disciplinary action which s/he faces. Here the rules are much clearer: the rights of the person facing disciplinary action are laid down, the time allowed for the accused to prepare their case is specified, notice is given of every stage in the disciplinary process, the make-up of the disciplinary panel is stated and the right of appeal is explained. Reading the procedures it seems as if the accused is now the centre of attention and the alleged victim is just an observer, watching from a distance.

The rules of natural justice must be followed and someone accused of sexual harassment or abuse is entitled to a fair process. However, the contrast in the procedures between the rights guaranteed to the accused and the relative absence of rights accorded to the complainant is startling. There was not much evidence of the 'procedural justice' which Vera Baird, the Victims Commissioner, told us is so important to a victim.

Perhaps there is an unstated assumption that the accused is at risk of suffering a punishment but the complainant has nothing to lose. Such an assessment is utterly wrong. The calumny which falls on a complainant if the accused escapes punishment is considerable and will inevitably be amplified by social media, as friends and supporters of the accused publicise the verdict and attack the complainant. If the disdain of colleagues is not penalty enough, the claimant will no doubt also remember that every procedure carries the threat of disciplinary action if a complainant is found to have 'maliciously' made a false accusation.

Tacked on

Most people will wonder how universities have managed to put themselves in this extraordinary position of operating procedures which demonstrate so little concern for the needs of complainants. The explanation is both sad and simple. Most university procedures were not constructed to deal with complaints of sexual harassment and abuse. They were developed at a time when sexual abuse was taken much less seriously and when almost all offences would have been of an entirely different nature. Even today, Students' Complaints and Disciplinary Procedures tend to focus on other issues. This list of examples comes from one of the universities which we described as traditionalist. Significantly, although this procedure is in current use, we can find no indication that it has been reviewed since it was first drafted over 10 years ago:

'Examples of circumstances that constitute gross misconduct include the following. This is not intended to be an exhaustive list.

- Stealing from the University or from staff or students of the University or from others on the premises.
- Destruction of, or serious damage to, University property or to a third party's property while on University property, or work related to the University.
- Violation of the safety policy of the University.
- Theft, fraud or deliberate falsification of records of or relating to the University
- Deliberately hacking or introducing a computer virus into the University's computer(s).
- Negligence that causes serious loss, damage or injury to the University or a fellow member of staff or fellow student.
- Serious harassment or bullying of a member of staff or fellow student of the University.

- Selling, distributing, possessing or using controlled substances or illegal drugs.
- Failure to declare a criminal conviction other than a conviction for minor motoring offences carrying a fixed penalty. (It will be at the discretion of the Director of School whether such matters need to be referred to a formal disciplinary panel. The Deputy Head of Student Support will act in an advisory capacity, as appropriate.)

Indulging in:

- Grossly insulting or abusive behaviour.
- Grossly obstructive or disruptive behaviour.
- Fighting or attempting to injure any person.
- Indecent behaviour.
- Unauthorised access, trespass on or occupation of University premises, including Halls of Residence, without the written permission or express consent of the University.
- Threatening or intimidating behaviour towards a student or member of staff of the University.
- Non-compliance with the disciplinary process.
- Serious misuse of University computer, intranet, internet and electronic mail systems which may for example:
  – cause damage or interruption to the system.
  – be threatening, intimidating, insulting or malicious.
  – affect the name or position of the University as a provider or user.
  – result in accessing or passing obscene material.
- Repeated commissions of acts of misconduct.'

Although there are references to people's behaviour and to 'serious bullying and harassment', it is notable that in a list of 18 examples, sexual harassment, sexual abuse and sexual assault are not mentioned. We were surprised that so many procedures use phrases like 'indecent behaviour', 'unwanted bodily contact' and 'violating another person's dignity' instead of naming specific sexual offences. This tentative tone seems out of place in the twenty-first century and seems to reflect an earlier time which disliked making explicit mention of sexual matters.

Alongside the complaints procedures are documents which set out the behaviour expected of students and staff. Most of these also seem to focus on the priorities of an earlier period. The student statements go into great detail about issues like accommodation, use of the library, laboratories and technical equipment. Sexual matters are typically dealt with in a more cursory fashion.

Staff statements usually speak of the need to behave with dignity and respect, but give few details of what this means in terms of sexual mores. Even in the more progressive and reforming universities, it is noticeable that while additions and amendments have been made to make clear, for instance, that sexual misconduct is a serious offence, the structure of their long-established procedural documents is often substantially unchanged.

It is hard to avoid the conclusion that these important procedures have not been remodelled and re-written to give a higher priority to sexual harassment and abuse. Instead, sexual matters have just been tacked on to old-fashioned documents whose focus remains elsewhere. The unfortunate result is that most universities have a set of procedures which might deal adequately with complaints about halls of residence being too cold in winter or misconduct which involves damage to university equipment but are not well designed to handle complaints of sexual harassment and abuse.

Sex between Staff and Students

Our research brought many surprises but, as we noted earlier, perhaps the greatest is that almost every university permits its teaching staff to have sex with students aged 18 years or over.[5]

In our FOI request we asked for:

- The guidance which the university gives to academic and non-academic staff in respect of sexual relationships with students.

The responses revealed no agreement about the attitude which universities should take. We discovered three different approaches:

- 45 universities (over 40% of the total) give **no explicit guidance** to their staff about sex with students.

    Some of these universities make general policy statements about maintaining professionalism and many warn their staff about conflicts of interest. But they stop short of advising their staff against sexual relationships with their students. Indeed, some universities seem content to see such relationships develop and leave it to each member of staff to ensure that a sexual relationship with a student is not exploitative. One university states:

    > 'It is recognised that the vast majority of students are aged 18 or over and therefore the University does not prevent staff and students developing relationships that may be romantic or sexual in nature however there is a duty to ensure that abuses of power do not occur and to guard against this and the perception of abuse of power.'

    This procedure does not explain how a member of staff avoids 'the perception of abuse of power' while having a sexual relationship with one of the students whom he or she teaches.

- 51 universities (half the total) make statements **discouraging or strongly discouraging** their teaching staff from having sex with students. Some of them explain that sexual relationships of this kind can be damaging to both parties and to the university. A typical statement reads:

> 'Staff members are warned that a sexual/romantic relationship with any student they are responsible for teaching, supervising or assessing is particularly sensitive as it compromises the professional relationship between staff and students, and potentially damages the teaching and learning environment for other students and staff members.'

However, having described the damage that can result from sex between staff and students, this university – like so many others – goes on to explain that such relationships are permitted.

> 'Although the University discourages such relationships in general and regards it as unprofessional for a staff member to actively seek to initiate such a relationship or to pursue such a relationship without regard to the problems which may ensue, it also recognises that human beings do become attracted to and involved with one another without deliberate intent and that such relationships may be genuinely affectionate, desired by both parties and impossible to stifle.'

Universities which take this approach require the member of staff to disclose the relationship to their manager, often on a special form. At which point the manager is expected to transfer the teaching and assessment of the student to another staff member, providing of course that this is feasible. No disciplinary issues arise unless a staff member fails to report a relationship, in which case disciplinary action 'may' be taken.

- 6 universities state that they take a more rigorous approach. They **prohibit sex** between staff and students in cases where the member of staff has some academic or managerial responsibility for the student.

    These six universities are:

    1. Greenwich University
    2. Lancaster University
    3. University of Leeds
    4. Nottingham Trent University
    5. University of Roehampton
    6. University College, London

As part of our survey of procedures in Oxford colleges, we also discovered that St Hugh's College and Oriel College have implemented a similar prohibition.

The difference between these three approaches is substantial. A sexual relationship which is permitted in some universities would lead to disciplinary action in several others. Moreover, these differences in approach suggest that there is a significant divergence of opinion about the extent of a university's legitimate authority and how it should exercise its duty of care towards students and members of staff. The implications of these disagreements are serious. If universities cannot even agree whether sexual relationships between staff and students meet acceptable standards of professionalism, equality and respect, it will be difficult to develop a sector-wide policy on sexual behaviour.

There is a further complication. We also asked universities for,

- The guidance which the university gives to students in respect of sexual relationships with employees of the university.

In this case, all universities gave the same answer. No university gives guidance to students about sex with members of staff and, as far as we know, none of the universities which discourages or prohibits staff from having sex with students has drawn that policy to the attention of students and none has explained how that policy could affect a student.[6] This seems a very regrettable oversight.

Assessment

In the last chapter we brought together a summary of recent university sexual scandals which have been reported in the national media. In this chapter we have uncovered important weaknesses in the procedures which universities use when dealing with complaints of sexual harassment and abuse. In the last section we have also explained that universities have very different responses to the question of whether their staff should have sex with their students.

In Chapter 3 we reported on our interviews with people from all parts of the university community. Almost everyone we interviewed told us that they do not have confidence in the current arrangements for handling sexual harassment and abuse. Our interviewees insisted that universities should give a higher priority to reducing sexual misconduct and should improve the manner in which they handle complaints. The evidence in this chapter provides substantial support for those views.

In later chapters we suggest the improvements which we believe are needed and consider how they might be brought about. However, before proposing a programme of reform, we will address the question of why sexual harassment and abuse is so common in our universities.

Appendix

Research into sexual abuse in universities

Freedom of Information Request

Dear (Executive Assistant to the Vice-Chancellor of ... University)

I will be grateful if you would pass this Freedom of Information request to the (Vice Chancellor). The following information is requested:

- The procedure which the university follows when a student makes a complaint of sexual abuse, sexual harassment or sexual assault.
- The procedure which the university follows when a member of the academic staff makes a complaint of sexual abuse, sexual harassment or sexual assault.
- The procedure which the university follows when a member of non-academic staff, makes a complaint of sexual abuse, sexual harassment or sexual assault.
- The guidance which the university gives to academic staff in respect of sexual relationships with students.
- The guidance which the university gives to non-academic staff in respect of sexual relationships with students.
- The guidance which the university gives to students in respect of sexual relationships with employees of the university.

By *academic staff*, I refer to employees whose normal duties involve teaching or research. By *non-academic staff*, I refer to employees whose normal duties are not primarily teaching or research.

The information is sought as part of research into sexual abuse in universities. My co-researcher is Eva Tutchell.

Thank you for your help.

Yours sincerely

John Edmonds

6

Living with the Market

Institutes of Higher Education are not divorced from the rest of society. As we were reminded by more than one person whom we interviewed, universities form part of British society and they reflect its culture.

The power structure in our society is still male dominated. So let us take a moment to consider what this means.

An Unequal Society

We found, when we wrote *ManMade*,[1] that men still hold 80% of the most powerful jobs in Britain. A similar imbalance exists in universities.

Nearly three quarters of the MPs in our Parliament are still men. In our largest companies, the Chief Executive and the Finance Director have the most powerful jobs. There are 700 of these top jobs in the FTSE 350. At the last count 657 of these 700 jobs were held by men and only 43 by women. This means that men occupy 94% of the main positions of power in British business.

There is much talk of the gender pay gap being narrowed, and it is true that the BBC has managed to reduce theirs to 10.7%. However many companies in the same sector have not even matched the BBC's slow progress. ITN's gender pay gap is 16.8%, and their bonus gap is a very large 60%.[2]

In the Arts, not only are there far fewer women theatre directors, they also suffer from a gender pay gap, and in research carried out by the Arts Council of Great Britain, the number of productions by women playwrights is falling.[3] Although more women than men graduate in art and design courses, men's exhibits far outnumber those of women in major art exhibitions.

Contrary to popular belief, only 36% of directors of charities are women. Although we now have more female solicitors and doctors, the top jobs in these fields are still occupied by men.

The lowest paid and part-time jobs are still mainly performed by women.

A similar pattern exists in higher education. In 2017–2018 only 26% of professors were women.[4] We were told by a union representative at one university that all the temporary staff are female.

Some Inhibiting Factors

Many women admit to suffering from the imposter syndrome: women doubting themselves and constantly looking over their shoulder to see if they will be found wanting. Even women as eminent and successful as the astronomer Jocelyn Bell Burnell confess to moments of self-doubt. When she was accepted to study for her PhD at Cambridge, she admitted in a radio programme:

> 'I kept thinking they've made a mistake. I should leave before they find me out.'[5]

Even more surprising, Ninette de Valois, in an interview when she was 82 years of age, with a history of decades of success in the world of dance, said,

> 'I kept waiting for them to find me out.'[6]

Every woman we interviewed for *ManMade*, all successful in their chosen field and some household names, told us that their reputation was due to luck – being in the right place at the right time, someone else noticing their ability.

From an early age girls are encouraged to be compliant, not to show anger, not to challenge men. As one well-known writer and campaigner said to us

> "I find it easier to be obliging."

Most women admit to the need to be liked, which can result in their seeking approval at times when they ought to be standing firm and asserting their rights. They wait for recognition rather than putting themselves forward for promotion. Sally Martin, a vice president of Shell told us:

> "If I was doing good work, that should be enough. Like many women I don't like promoting myself and rarely think of doing so."[7]

The few women who make it to the top of their profession are usually scrutinised to a degree never experienced by men. It is almost a truism by now that what are considered qualities in male leaders are severely criticised when exercised by women.

The evidence is clear: we live in an unequal society. The power structure determines the culture, so it is not surprising that many men have a sense of entitlement to privilege and that many women doubt their own abilities.

Inequality in Universities

Most people would assume that institutes of higher education, places where teaching and learning in a congenial atmosphere is taken for granted, are immune to the unequal norms which surround them.

However, our research into sexual harassment and abuse indicates unquestionably that this is not the case.

A former senior staff member at a prestigious university told us:

> "The power play at universities echoes the power play in society."

The determination of government is that universities become more like private sector companies with the same obsession with financial returns and the same tendency to neglect the human values of empathy and mutual support. The university is the corporation, the academic staff are somewhat insecure employees and the students are customers, whose demands must be satisfied.[9]

This approach was exemplified by a Minister for Higher Education who announced that the value of degrees should be judged by the earning power of graduates, with those on higher salaries deemed more successful. Where does this utilitarian attitude leave teachers, nurses and artists?

Although women hold 49% of faculty positions, only 38% are in tenured jobs. The average earnings of male professors are 12% more than that of women at the same level of seniority. 67.52% of part-time posts are held by women in universities.[8] We seem to be taking the same path as the United States where one study found that university student perceptions are that 'women are teachers, men are professors'.[10]

A myth persists that universities are different – bastions of liberal humanitarian values in a harsh and unsympathetic world. As a senior member of staff said to us sadly:

> "The concept of universities as a community of scholars has disappeared."

She was certainly not alone in holding that opinion.

There appears to be general agreement that the main difference in ambience and attitudes in universities in recent years is connected to the fact that funding now comes solely from student fees.

> "Students," said one lecturer, "have become an economic resource."

This new funding arrangement has led to a fundamental shift in many ways – not least because it tends to be tied to league tables. Universities are increasingly finding themselves strapped for cash, so that dominating the agenda at meetings of governing bodies and university councils is the need to raise funds. Managing the budget rather than managing people becomes the main focus of attention. As a member of one university governing body said to us

> "Although we read and hear reports on a wide range of subjects, sexual misconduct and abuse is not given any 'air time'."

Aware of the money that their university education now costs them and their parents, students have become more demanding, often disputing their grades, expressing dissatisfaction with the standard of their courses and feeling free to complain (sometimes, to be fair, with reason) if they are not given enough individual attention. However, their reactions are not always appropriate. We were told that students are very quick to criticise if lectures are cancelled, even when reasons are given for the cancellation and a substitute lecture is offered. The most laughable complaint we heard was when a student said he was shocked that a – very seasoned and respected – academic delivered her hour long lecture without recourse to notes!

Professor Alison Phipps of Sussex University is sure that universities have been infected by neoliberalism, which she describes as

> '...a value system in which the economic has replaced the intellectual and the political' and where 'Higher Education is seen as a skills supply' where 'students are seen as consumers and academics as dispensers of a commodity'.[11]

Marketisation

Several commentators are concerned about what they call the 'marketisation' of universities. Institutions are promoted on the basis of results and students' future prospects. Areas of study which appeal on the grounds of utility rather than intellectual breadth are advocated. We are witnessing the demise of subjects such as philosophy, sociology, history, languages and the Arts. Science, technology, engineering, and mathematics (STEM) subjects are incontestably vital to the future prosperity of the country, but losing areas of the curriculum which help us to reflect and engage with issues that affect all of humanity stunts our imagination.

Debate ceases to be encouraged and there are fewer discussions about values.

A hierarchical structure exacerbates the situation, leading to greater unhelpful competitiveness, not only between universities but between schools of study within them. An adversarial culture is not conducive to the sensitivity necessary for the consideration of students' welfare. A National Union of Students research paper published in 2013 found that the outsourcing of services usually means a decline in support from university staff and often resulting in a change to a generally less caring ethos.[12]

The removal of the cap on student numbers in 2014 has led inevitably to competition between universities to boost their rolls. Inducements of all kinds are offered in order to coax students to their doors. It is all about 'bums on seats' rather than the value to the students. But university is not for everyone and the drop-out rate in some subjects is higher than expected. There is a 10% drop in computing, despite the pressure exerted on school leavers to pursue this area of study, extolling its vital place in a modern world.

Added to this mix is the lack of security of tenure for many university teaching staff. Most will have gone through the process of first, second and third degrees, progressing through post-doctoral research (described as 'slave labour' by one former student) where they are earning a pittance, before they are eligible to apply for posts as lecturers. Competition is fierce but when they finally secure a position it is often on a short term contract of one or two years. In some cases their teaching load is so large that they are unable to carry on with their own research.

We were told that teaching hours for PhD students in some universities have been reduced to zero hours contracts.

Such insecurity inevitably causes tensions and contributes to a generally unhappy environment of resentment and a limited desire to be involved in caring for others. Student and staff welfare is a casualty in this new regime, and this will even extend to those who are known to have suffered assault. In the majority of universities, there is no full-time appointment with responsibility for dealing with such cases. Part-time positions exist, but they are on temporary contracts or have teaching commitments as well, so cannot devote the time or energy needed to deal with issues that are time consuming.

The University Environment

Going to university takes many young people away from home for the first time. The freedom of university life can be exciting, but much else is new and confusing: there is no immediate family support and no network of trusted friends. In their first year in particular, many students can feel lonely. A student in his first term told us that some of his fellow undergraduates, who come from small communities or from a very protective family home, can feel bewildered by the social life on campus and beyond. They have never been 'clubbing' for instance and are unsure what is expected of them.

> "They have no education on going out etiquette and some of the eighteen year old boys start to push and shove competing to see who has the sharpest elbows."

They will find themselves living in university accommodation or sharing a flat with strangers. They are probably not used to caring for themselves, being responsible for cooking, shopping, cleaning as well as studying for their degree. Of course most young students adapt quickly to their new life as adults, free to make their own decisions and learning from their mistakes. This is all part of growing up.

The difference between the life of students and their counterparts who are earning money is that they are living in a closed community. If you are studying at a campus university, almost everything is provided for you in terms of entertainment, health services, sports facilities, shops and limited transport. With this amount of convenience, students probably feel cushioned against some of the risks faced by those studying in large towns or cities.

However, even universities in a metropolis are to some extent closed communities. The ivory tower metaphor may be an exaggeration but these institutions are cut off from the outside world. The opportunity to study with few interruptions, where quiet contemplation and orderly debate takes place, is rightly valued and protected. But to whom are they answerable if serious offences, such as sexual abuse, are committed? The instinct, as we have seen, often seems to be the preservation of the reputation of the university above any real inspection of the incident. This is a society largely hidden from scrutiny. Criticism is resented and usually ignored. Unfortunately this complacency sustains a culture which in some respects is pernicious and damaging.

We need also to consider something that was mentioned to us several times: the concept of universities as 'liberal' institutions where freedom of expression is paramount. This implies allowing any members of a university to think and behave in ways that are free from what are seen as old fashioned prejudice: any questioning of such attitudes is considered an infringement of a sacrosanct liberty. If behaviour goes beyond acceptable boundaries, this has to be viewed as part of enlightened free thinking, and if a problem arises, the university itself can deal with it. It is not difficult to envisage how such a powerful belief system can leave abuses to fester.

The situation is made worse because of the sensitivity of the issue of sexual harassment and abuse and the need for confidentiality. Several people used almost identical words to us:

> "Matters are dealt with behind closed doors to protect the reputation of the university."

Sexual Harassment and Abuse in Higher Education

The National Union of Students survey in 2010[13] – the first of its kind – asked all women members of the NUS about their experience of sexual and physical abuse, harassment and assault. 2058 women responded: 94% were full time, 88% were from the UK and 86% were younger than 25 years.

68% have been subject to some form of physical or sexual abuse like groping, flashing or unpleasant comments. Sometimes university staff were involved. Young students were found to be particularly vulnerable. 87% of incidents took place in their first or second year.

A third of respondents feel unsafe in the campus in the evening. Halls of residence are regarded as unsafe because security is inadequate and security staff are often unsympathetic.

> 'Security is entirely unconcerned with the welfare of young women. They are liable to regard young women in distress as drunk with no thought that they may nevertheless need help and maybe their drink has been spiked.'

Reporting levels of incidents is low – 40% told no one, 21% told the university and 17% told the police.

Reasons given for not reporting ranged from feeling that the incident was not serious enough, they felt shame and embarrassment (including 50% victims of serious assault) or fear of being blamed or not believed. A big concern was not letting family, friends and partners find out.

Very worryingly, according to research conducted by The Empowered Campus and featured on their website, 71% of male students who are assaulted deal with their distress entirely alone.[14]

Sexual harassment and abuse may be even more prevalent in universities than in British society. Indeed Dame Vera Baird, The Victims' Commissioner for England and Wales said, in a recent radio interview that the incidence of rape in universities was twice that in society outside.

We have to assume therefore that there must be features of the university environment which make the incidence in higher education worse than in Britain generally.

Vera Baird told us that when reports of abuse are received and university authorities decide to take disciplinary action, there is still a lack of expertise to conduct these matters.

The Lad Culture

The 'Lad Culture', as described by Alison Phipps, is an

> '...unattractive feature of current university life.' [15]

Young men who feel that their masculinity is under threat in this more enlightened age of greater equality for women, parade their 'virility' in a variety of ways – most of which would be pathetic if they did not target women and other vulnerable members of the university community.

Often it begins with 'banter': jokey comments aimed at women, which the men see as harmless fun. This can escalate into unpleasant jibes and insults which some women have said that they are able to brush off with a firm response. However, these offensive remarks can then step up a gear, becoming crude and lewd and even menacing, especially if the caller is accompanied by his cronies. The recipient often feels exposed and helpless.

Alison Phipps gives examples of how lad culture is dominating the social sphere of university life:

- Rugby teams wearing Tee shirts saying 'Campus Rapist';
- A member of a feminist society locked in a coach toilet and pelted with porn magazines;

- In Durham University, members dressed as Jimmy Savile, his victims and the police;
- 'With that lipstick you'd make my cock look like a barber's pole', shouted to a girl;
- A woman was pushed downstairs in a bus for confronting a group exposing their penises;
- 'Fuck a Fresher' race;
- In a *Uni-lad* magazine, they wrote: '85% of rape cases go unreported – these are good odds';
- Seal clubbing – a repulsive term describing attacks on women Freshers.

Almost everyone we interviewed, men and women, spoke to us about the toxic atmosphere that is created when a sports club ethos gets out of hand. Rugby clubs were mentioned over and over again. On match days rowdy club members and hangers-on will sometimes deliberately drink to excess and harass and abuse women in the way we describe in Chapter 2.

Robert Hogg, a lecturer in Australian studies, writes,

> 'Contact sports like rugby need to be recognized for what they are; ritualized and repetitive displays of hypermasculinity, staged by men for men.'[16]

No doubt this view of an internationally popular sport will be hotly disputed, but the behaviour of some university teams and their fans does nothing to contradict this opinion. Their behaviour is then shared on social media, and typically it is the victim who is blamed or sneered at.

In October 2014, the LSE rugby team was suspended from playing for the rest of the academic year after calling the female students 'slags' and 'mingers' in a leaflet handed out at a Freshers' Fair. It also offered advice on getting drunk and 'pulling' an ugly woman. An investigation was launched after the university received complaints about the leaflet.

Nona Buckley-Irvine, the General Secretary of LSE Student Union, said that the language was not merely banter.

> 'What we have in this leaflet is content that mocks a woman, mocks women in sport, mocks people for their sexual orientation. We can't tolerate things that seek to perpetrate the existing culture of misogyny and sexism.'[17]

The rugby club has admitted that the leaflet contained 'offensive and stigmatising language'.[18]

An interesting comment was made to us by a union representative of another London university:

> "Women's rugby here is taking on toxic male culture but the women's roller skating team is not, so it is not inevitable".

In a 2019 article on lad culture, Alison Phipps further clarifies the concept of what is meant by 'lads'. She reminds us that Paul Willis's iconic study *Learning to Labour*, published in 1977, describes 'the lads',

> '…as working class boys 'rebelling against academia for constructing them as failures.'

In fact as Alison Phipps points out:

> 'The main players in the recent theatre of students' laddism in the UK appear to be mainly middle class and white.'[19]

In chapter 2 we gave examples of the effects of alcohol on a group of young men and showed how their language coarsened as they became steadily more drunk.[20] An aspect that has not so far been much mentioned is the homophobia which lies behind their comments. The conversation of this group began to focus more and more on the penis, illustrating male anxieties about size and performance. Gay men were despised and ridiculed, referred to as poofs and queers, but more graphically as 'turd burglars' and 'chutney ferrets'.

As the writers of this article say:

> 'These definitions distance homosexuality and strengthen hegemonic masculinity.'[21]

Reports from the NUS and UUK tell us that LGBT students are even more vulnerable to abuse than others.

Richard Taulke-Johnson writes about aspects of the life of gay and lesbian students, including how their sexuality even influences their choice of university and accommodation.[22]

Pornography

The current easy access to porn has already been referred to and probably has more effect on the minds of viewers than they realise. The portrayal of women in porn is that of submissive women smiling and apparently enjoying their degradation. It sets a dangerous level of unreal sexual expectation in the men who watch it.

According to Kat Banyard,

> 'The scale on which pornography is now consumed, overwhelmingly by heterosexual men and boys, strips away any pretences pornographers or porn watchers might once have had of representing a shunned 'counterculture.''[23]

In England, according to research conducted by a team from the Universities of Central Lancashire and Bristol, 39% of boys aged 14–17 years regularly watch pornography. Yet concern about its effect is dismissed by some as harmless fantasy.

> 'My 13 year old son is watching porn on his tablet. Should I be worried?' asks an anxious mother.[24]

In answer, a report from the Children's Commissioner shows that this mother most definitely should. This report considers the impact of pornography on children and young people and states

> '...pornography influences attitudes towards relationships and sex.'[25]

In an article in *Psychology Today*, Alexandra Katehatis writes:

> 'Sadly pornography paints an unrealistic picture of sexuality and relationships that can create an expectations for real life experiences that will never be fulfilled.'[26]

To quote Kat Banyard again:

> 'Pornography denotes a trade in which real live women – not imaginary women, not fantasy women – are paid ... to have sex at prescribed times, with prescribed people, for prescribed durations in prescribed ways.'[27]

Young male university students, perhaps themselves inexperienced in sexual relationships, are likely to be literally seduced into thinking not only that these demeaning practices are what women desire but are what gives them pleasure. A male student told us that,

> "Porn viewing definitely results in a lowering of standards in how women should be treated and a rise in false expectations of sexual encounters."

Predators on the Teaching Staff

So far in this chapter we have concentrated on harassment and abuse within the student community but, as outlined in a Chapter 2, perpetrators of assault are not confined to undergraduates. A few members of the teaching staff at all levels – from junior lecturers to professors (some eminent) are known to indulge in abusive practices.

Because sexual abuse is not always regarded as a serious problem, abusers, often serial offenders, feel they can act with impunity. It is important to stress that perpetrators are often guilty of systematic multiple misdemeanors. Unfortunately, however, every case that comes to light is usually regarded by the university as a 'one off', so cumulative evidence is not taken into account. This gives the impression that all is well except for a few occasional infringements. Universities also fear the disruption caused by disciplinary procedures and, even more, by the fact that the stories might be pounced on by the media.

What Leila Whitley and Tiffany Page[28] call 'the slipperiness of sexism' means that a culture which is hostile to women remains unchallenged. We are therefore forced to conclude that institutional misogyny is to blame. A harsh verdict, but from the evidence of interviews we have conducted, official reports published by UUK, UCU and NUS and research carried out by concerned academics, such a conclusion seems to be inescapable.

A Freedom of Information request to 120 universities by the *Guardian* found that between 2011–2012 and 2016–2017, 169 allegations of assault were made by students and at least 127 allegations about staff were made by colleagues.[29]

In *The Guardian* article, Dr Ann Olivearius, senior partner at the law firm McAllister Olivarius, is quoted as saying

> 'Sexual harassment of students by staff members has reached epidemic levels in British universities... disciplinary action is pretty much nonexistent. Those in charge are often colleagues who have many incentives not to intervene.'

A cause for grave concern is that when this report was published in 2017 only four UK universities openly declared rape and sexual assault to be grounds for extenuating circumstances, which means a pause in their studies or special consideration in taking examinations. So victims of trauma could be forced to choose between continuing their studies or dropping out regardless of emotional distress.

In this culture the complainant can find herself the butt of irritation from her peers when charges of assault

> '...can get in the way of institutional happiness.'[30]

Anger is expressed about the disruption of studies rather than sympathy with the victim/survivor.

We should stress that many students do not find themselves exposed to harassment or abuse and may even deny its existence on campus, but this does not make it any less essential to examine the culture that encourages perpetrators to commit what sometimes amount to criminal offences.

It might be useful to inspect more closely what is happening that makes such a sorry situation possible.

Managers and Leaders

We were told that although heads of department and heads of schools of study are experts in their own academic field, some whose reputation stretches beyond academe, most have no managerial training or experience. Their leadership skills may be learnt in haphazard fashion as they progress through the ranks, but this method does not guarantee the necessary wisdom and knowledge about managing people.

In institutes of higher education, as in the commercial world, courses advertising leadership abound. It is revealing to explore how leadership is defined and promoted. The qualities which are top of any list on such courses tend to be honesty, integrity, communication skills, listening skills, creativity, the ability to delegate and resilience.

Lesley Wilkin, the UK managing Director of Hay, the Human Resources consultants, describes what is needed in a leader. She says that good leaders must be

> "...adept at managing the complex relationships with the many stakeholders of an organisation."[31]

Annie Pye, University of Exeter agrees. Her own research demonstrates that successful leaders operate

> "...at the centre of a web of relationships."[32]

This is the sensible and enlightened theory. However, in practice the qualities which seem to be admired in leaders in business and in politics consist instead of being tough risk takers, blunt, determined, ruthless and unwavering.

An article in the *Independent* refers to the way Donald Trump is regarded.

'He's a real leader. Always gets his way. Won't take no for an answer... These qualities of pushiness, selfishness, deceptiveness are not just excused in such men. They are valued.'[33]

Mark Zuckerberg is Chairman and Chief Executive of Facebook.

Scott Galloway, a NYU professor, says that,

'Mark Zuckerberg is the most dangerous person in the world'[34]

The UK and Canadian Parliaments joined forces to request Zuckerberg's attendance at the House of Commons DCMS select committee in an attempt to question him about Facebook's role in the Cambridge Analytica scandal. These governments were later joined by Argentina, Australia and Ireland. Zuckerberg replied that he had

'...not time to speak to every country's law makers'.

This response shows not only complete lack of understanding of the genuine worries expressed about the 'fake news' apparently spread on Facebook during an election campaign, but breathtaking arrogance. These are hardly the actions of a responsible leader.

Martin Sorrell, until recently CEO of WPP, the largest advertising conglomerate in the world, is now CEO of S4 Capital. In a *Guardian* article, the *Financial Times* is quoted saying that Sorrell

'...had a reputation for bullying junior staff and creating a toxic environment and a fear culture.'[35]

To reinforce this judgment, the newspaper recalled that,

'He sacked his chauffeur after his driver refused to start work at 7 a.m., having driven Sorrell's wife home at 2 a.m. the same morning'.

The *Independent* article wonders whether the leadership style of men like Trump and Harvey Weinstein is connected to the abuse of which they have both been accused.

> 'We need to reassess how the professional qualities which we endorse might well align with the sexual abuse we excuse.'[36]

What has for years been acknowledged to be rife in the film industry, but only since the rise of the #MeToo movement openly seen to be despicable, is also present in our universities.

At the beginning of this chapter we gave examples to illustrate areas of inequality between men and women in Britain in the twenty-first century. Gains have been fought for and won, but not in every aspect of our lives.

Month after month we read, hear and see in the media that rape cases go unreported, are withdrawn and the alleged perpetrators are not convicted. In London in 2018–2019 only 1.5% reports of rape resulted in a suspect being charged or summoned. Of the cases which are sent for trial, only 3% result in convictions. One woman was raped by a stranger who was identified eight years later as raping again. She was told by police that in order to charge him they would have to go through her school and university records, medical records and about six years of therapy notes.[37] It is no wonder that victims withdraw from such a process.

There are few reported cases of actual rape in universities, because any victim who has been raped, already traumatized by the experience, is going to think twice about submitting herself to such an ordeal.

We were sad to find that for women the atmosphere in some universities is often uninviting and, at worst, it can be intimidating.

Human Resources

We asked many interviewees whether the Human Resources (HR) department in their universities had been helpful. The response was almost universally condemnatory. A victim/survivor we interviewed did tell us that one member of her HR department had taken considerable trouble to put her in touch with relevant people who could take her case forward. Unfortunately this diligent person was moved to another department soon after. Apart from this single exception, the general feeling was that HR had been extremely unhelpful, obstructive and even unpleasant.

Here is a taste of what we were told – every example from a different university:

> "… HR sees its role as looking after management and encouraging a repressive regime where people are told to shut up."
>
> (Interviewee looking horrified) "I've never been so depressed about it. I'd have committed suicide if I had to work in HR."
>
> "They are very unhelpful when advising on job security."
>
> (Making what we began to describe as the 'HR face'.) "They do nothing."
>
> (Eyes rolling to the heavens.) "They are appalling, not collaborative or supportive"
>
> "They are often ruthless, inefficient and generally unpleasant"
>
> "They are stooges: spectacularly incompetent and constantly making errors."

> "They are tools of management."
>
> "HR don't seem to be informed about our policies."
>
> "Because of the complexity of academic rights, HR tends to be very reluctant to take a position on cases affecting academics and they often harbour outdated attitudes to expected student behaviour."

And at last, the one positive comment:

> "The HR management were very helpful and gave a lot of assistance."

These strong negative reactions tell their own story. Officially HR is not responsible for what happens after a charge of sexual assault in universities, but these criticisms imply an unwarranted and unsympathetic attitude to people in distress.

Conclusion

In summarising the areas covered in this chapter, we are forced to the conclusion that the quality of life in many universities is not as happy or as fulfilled as it could and, indeed, should be.

Gender inequality in staff appointments, constant concerns about funding, a utilitarian approach to success caused by league tables and a hierarchical structure lead to low morale and distrust.

Insecurity of tenure causes more anxiety among the teaching staff, who find themselves overworked and with less time to devote to their own emotional needs and those of their students. This situation is exacerbated by the outsourcing of services.

'Lad' culture and the toxic ethos surrounding some rugby and other sports clubs when team members and followers are fuelled by alcohol are responsible for aggressive and even abusive behaviour.

Action against predatory staff abusing their power is neither swift nor strong enough to deter recurrences and leadership, and management qualities among senior staff tend to be variable.

Accounts we heard, almost without exception, condemning the lack of concern expressed or the even deliberately unhelpful attitudes demonstrated by HR departments, are grounds for serious concern.

We have painted a sorry picture, but in the next chapter we consider some reasons for this state of affairs in universities and give some encouraging examples of good practice.

7

Seeking a Better Culture

It seems to us that the greatest contributory factor to the abusive behaviour we are witnessing in universities is a toxic masculinity. Misogyny and a confusion about sex, power and dominance add to this pernicious climate.

If the assertion made to us that universities mirror society is valid, then part of our recourse must be to attempt to change the prevailing culture we live in. This entails challenging some deeply held values and beliefs.

We are aware of the difficulty of such an undertaking: when we talk about 'culture' we are implying a whole way of life and socially accepted and deeply ingrained tenets of behaviour.

Society is responsible for the feelings of alienation in some men and it is difficult to change stereotypes. However, we should take heart from the fact that there is a growing understanding among many men that this is not the way life should be. There is a capacity for change and this needs to be seized.

Let us consider how men think they need to be seen and contrast this with how they might actually see themselves. It is worth taking a moment to reflect on the causes of these often conflicting notions.

Men and Masculinity

The first point to emphasise is that masculinity is a socially constructed identity. Whatever sex we are born into there is a gendering process and 'gender roles in our society are rigidly defined and vigilantly enforced'.[1] However, it is important, as the feminist Lynne Segal warns,[2] that we do not simply equate masculinity with dominance. It is much more complicated than that.

It has long been recognised that baby boys and girls are socialised differently: evidence tells us that even today the girl is rocked gently and cooed over, the boy more likely to be jiggled and thrown in the air.[3] Cards congratulating the proud parents on their new arrival will feature little girls dressed in pink and looking coy while the boys will be wearing blue and engaged in kicking a ball about or other 'manly' sports. The illustrations on these cards show girls more often than not sitting and static, the boys on the move and taking up space. This is followed by the marketing of toys considered more appropriate for boys or girls. Dolls, prams and cooking implements for girls with building bricks and guns for boys.

Boys are often discouraged from showing too much emotion. An exception is made for success on sports fields, when open displays of physical affection abound. Indeed as Lynne Segal says,

> 'the constant pressure to confirm masculinity in its difference from femininity may explain why it is only when men are at their unquestionably masculine, like footballers in action, they embrace, weep and display such behaviour'.[4]

Boys and men are told to 'man up', 'have balls', 'not be a sissy' (i.e. not behave like a girl). Such repeated admonitions have the effect of diminishing and narrowing the horizons of boys into a restricted manhood. The powerful underlying message is to persuade young men and boys to distance themselves from any thought or gesture with feminine overtones. It is very hard for young men to resist such conditioning.

The obvious corollary is that generations of men grow up feeling the need to express their masculinity by at least pretending to appear emotionally tough, physically strong and with an ambivalent attitude towards feminine qualities. Peer pressure – especially through social media – to conform to this hard-edged, insensitive stereotype of what it means to be a man must inevitably take its toll.

If we take this a step further, it becomes easy to understand why some men have little respect for and, in the worst scenario, even contempt for women.

When this sense of apparently unconditional entitlement is thwarted it can lead to the anger and consequent abuse with which this book is concerned.

The Sexuality of Men

The Sexuality of Men, edited by Andy Metcalfe and Martin Humphries, was published in 1985 and widely read and commented on at that time.[5] Sadly their words still resonate a generation later.

The essays in their book are all written by men who perceive and understand how men cope with their sexual identities and their fears. All the writers have some sympathy with the anxieties and conflicting feelings of men. They worry about their role in society and how this is expressed through sexual relations with women.

However, the authors do not shy away from criticising what they call 'evasive action' when it comes to confronting the subject of sexual violence.

> 'When we have begun to think about our own behaviour and how we are implicated in violence', writes Tony Eardley, 'we are often confused, defensive, self-doubting or self-hating and resentful. A challenge to sexual violence may itself produce a further violent reaction'.

From Darwin, through to Konrad Lorenz's thesis in *On Aggression* and Desmond Morris's *The Naked Ape,* an assumption is made about men's innate and uncontrollable aggressive tendencies.

Shere Hite's 1981 report on men and sexuality[6] concludes that for men

> 'validation (of their sex and gender) is gained through sex. It shores up a sense of maleness.'

Furthermore Shere Hite's report tells us, with the evidence gained from hundreds of interviews, that male sexuality is repeatedly equated with the penis. And this might go some way towards explaining some of the insecurity men feel about their potency.

> 'The penis seems to have a life of its own – over which a man does not have full control.'

Adolescent boys' obsession with their penis and genitals can be corroborated by any teacher of that age group. One of us (Eva) taught in two single-sex secondary boys' schools and can attest to the fact that any textbook was liberally decorated with drawings of male genitalia – often of exaggerated proportions.

Elizabeth Wilson in *What is to be done about violence against women*[7] says:

> 'Biology becomes a giant moral let-out. Such arguments are popular because they pander to our inertia. After all, to change one's behaviour involves pain and effort. It's much easier to pretend to be a baboon.'

However, this lack of control over their penis should not be used as an excuse, as it sometimes is, for not taking responsibility for sexual abuse.

This reminds us of the famous rebuke that an American judge apparently delivered when a defendant, who was accused of rape, said he could not resist temptation because the girl was wearing a short skirt. The judge gave him short shrift:

> 'No man ever died of a terminal erection.'

In Lynne Segal's book[8] over 100 pages are given over to the consideration of how men behave sexually. The dominant feature of their masculinity appears to be dictated by sexual relationships. She writes with sympathy for men who are endeavouring to free themselves from this one-dimensional concept of manhood, quoting from Pleck and Sawyer's seminal text *Men and Masculinity*.[9]

> 'Some of us are searching for new ways to work that will more fully express ourselves rather than our learned desire for masculinity.'

Over 40 years later that search still continues.

Pornography

The widespread use of pornography has already been discussed in the previous chapter. It is now big business and, as hinted in Chapter 2, it fuels anxiety about performance in its male viewers; anxieties about clumsiness, inadequacy and tension about 'doing it right'.

> 'It is in the space between this anxiety and fantasy realm of a perfect world that pornography achieves its power...'[10]

There is no interest or concern about a woman's satisfaction in pornographic images and films. It is all based on the very male assumption that she enjoys everything which is done to her.

JJ Bola puts it succinctly:

> '... misogyny and rape culture thrive off the idea that men are entitled to women's bodies'[11]

In an article in *The Telegraph*,[12] Charles Hymas, their Home Affairs Editor, tells us that according to research carried out by the British Board of Film Classification, children, boys and girls as young as seven are viewing porn online. Many said they had come across 'extreme, aggressive or violent porn' which they found upsetting and disturbing. All the young people interviewed said that it had changed their attitude to sex. Most said it made them disrespectful of the opposite sex. Worryingly, three quarters of the parents interviewed claimed their children had not seen porn online but over half (53%) of their own children said they had viewed it.

Violence and Sexuality

In her book *Pimp State: Sex money and the future of equality*,[13] based on interviews with sex workers and also many women and men involved in taking part in pornographic films, Kat Banyard comes to the conclusion that,

> 'to use pornography is to use women as if they were instruments.'

She quotes a male porn actor who tells her what happens to women porn actors:

> 'they start fucking the woman about 2 p.m. and go on till midnight'.

This comment should quell any proponents of the notion that pornography somehow empowers the women who are taking part.

Kat Banyard's conclusion, citing research carried out over four decades, is that the effect of men's use of pornography leads to what she terms 'psychological desensitisation' and that porn inspires,

> 'misogynistic beliefs and sexist violence'.

When the real women, wives and girlfriends, with whom men have sexual relations, do not seem to live up to the distorted 'ideal' of feminine perfection of the women in the porn films, they often show their disappointment or disgust by punishing their partners. We saw in Chapter 2 how Durham University students meted out abusive treatment to what are deemed as 'ugly' girls and women.

Precarious Masculinity

It would be ludicrous to blame women for not coming up to the required standard, and therefore excusing the behaviour of abusive men. Clearly that would be grossly unfair.

However, that is the temptation. We cannot ignore the fact as one man put it that,

> 'masculinity is never something that we can feel at ease with. It is always something we have to be ready to prove and defend.'[14]

Metcalfe and Humphries pose the question,

> 'So what is this masculinity which is so powerful and dominant but also apparently fragile and vulnerable to challenge?'[15]

An answer to this question would help society to begin to address issues ranging from general inequality to sexual harassment, abuse and violence.

Misogyny

Misogyny is derived from the Greek word 'misogunia', meaning hatred of women. It has a long history.

A few examples:

Aristotle described woman as an, 'incomplete male'.

Joshua Swetman, a seventeenth-century English fencing master, wrote,

> 'Women are crooked by nature.... Going all the way back to Eve, womankind was no sooner made but straightway her mind was set upon mischief'.

A more recent example is of Jack Semple, a Boston Marathon official, trying to forcibly remove Kathrine Switzer, the first woman to take part in the race in 1967. In a previous book, *Man Made: Why so few women are in positions of power*,[16] we told the story of the sports commentator, John Inverdale, whose response when Marion Bartoli won the Wimbledon Singles Title in 2013, was,

> 'She's never going to be a looker'.

After angry criticism, he gave a rather perfunctory apology saying his comment had been misinterpreted and, anyway, he was suffering from hay fever on that day.

In the summer of 2019 onlookers were horrified to see Conservative MP Mark Field physically ejecting a woman Greenpeace protester from a Mansion House banquet, grabbing her by the neck.[17]

A video[18] showing nine male pastors of the United Church quoting sexist and misogynistic comments all made by male prelates to female clerics exemplifies the problem in that Church.

> 'I can't concentrate on your sermon because you are so pretty.'
>
> 'This is our little girl preacher.'
>
> 'If God can use a donkey, I guess he can use women in the ministry.'
>
> 'If I were 20 years younger, you wouldn't be able to keep me away from you.'
>
> As one of the more enlightened pastors exclaims in exasperation:
>
> 'For too long, both inside and outside the Church, transformational accountability hasn't been practised.'

Many commentators have suggested that Boris Johnson epitomises the careless misogyny which underlies the kind of taken-for-granted male privilege that is exhibited by some students arriving at universities. He commented on MPs working through September as being 'girly swots' and described Jeremy Corbyn as 'a big girl's blouse'.

Johnson's biographer, Sonia Purnell,[19] tells us that,

> 'in his writing women were portrayed as 'bubbling blondes.'

Homosexuals are referred to as 'bumboys'. His Islamophobic remarks were specifically aimed at women wearing burkas: calling them 'bank robbers' or 'looking like letterboxes'. About all of these accusations, he appears completely unrepentant.

Considering the accumulated evidence, it is not hard to agree with Kalpana Srivastava et al. when they write:

> 'Misogyny has taken shape in multiple forms such as male privilege, patriarchy, gender discrimination, sexual harassment, belittling of women and violence against women.'[20]

This is the world which universities inhabit.

It is worth pointing out that we are concentrating on the behaviour of some heterosexual men. From official reports by the National Union of Students (NUS)[21] and Universities UK (UUK)[22] we learn that LGBT students and staff are also at risk of abuse and clearly not all men fit into the masculine stereotype we have described.

Indeed, as the gay black American writer, Julius Lester, rather sadly comments:

> 'I tried to believe my parents when they told me I was a boy, but I could find no objective proof for such an assertion.'[23]

It is also important to stress that we are not in any way suggesting that all or indeed most men are guilty of the reprehensible actions we have heard about from the many women who volunteered to speak to us. Indeed we can imagine some angry or anguished readers exclaiming, 'I am nothing like this', or, 'My son/husband is gentle, caring and would never behave so disreputably'. Some might even say, 'I don't recognize most of the men I know in what you are writing'.

Of course there are many exceptions. Nevertheless the painful fact remains that the behaviour of a good number of men in universities is creating a toxic climate in which sexual harassment and abuse is commonplace.

Moreover, if this blight in our institutions is to be eradicated, we will need the collaboration of men. We will need men to challenge existing and damaging notions of masculinity and create a benign culture which is more conducive for work and study.

We feel encouraged by the words of one enlightened man:

> 'As individuals we have the power to question what we have been taught, examine how we perpetuate this cycle and encourage others to do the same... We are not ciphers, and we make choices for which we are responsible and should be held responsible...'[24]

Hopeful Signs

Before turning directly to universities and what they might do to change the culture in their institutions, let us take a moment to look at what is going on in the world outside that gives us some hope.

Iman Amrani is a journalist for *The Guardian* newspaper who is currently writing articles about men and masculinity and how men feel about the way they are generally depicted.[25] She has also made some YouTube features which throw up some fascinating observations made by men aged between 13 and 60 years from various social classes and ethnicities.

She visits a barber shop where she finds hairdressers and clients with surprisingly honest opinions.

According to one barber, their salon was considered a safe place for men to talk and to express themselves:

> 'We can tap into what they want to speak about, how they deal with heartbreak for instance. Making connections.'

Another hairdresser said,

> 'Most of the time men want to feed their ego – all the bullshit. This is not how you want to be viewed.'

He continued,

> 'We need to have uncomfortable conversations.'

According to one teenager Iman Amrani interviewed, masculinity is defined by,

> 'How much you drink and how many women you have slept with.'

In answer to Iman's question, what does it mean to be a man, the first response was,

> 'Protecting your family and standing up for yourself.'

But then he added,

> 'Masculinity is not what you see on TV.'

His friend amplified this statement that young men want to be able to show their fears;

> 'How am I going to fit in?', and, 'am I going to make friends?'

We would contend that this vulnerability is echoed by the majority of teenagers, boys and girls. Feeling free to talk openly to one another about these very natural concerns would benefit the young people involved and society in general. More openness is always to be welcomed.

And the same applies to the staff and students of our universities.

An article by three Melbourne University academics[26] describes recently released guidelines from The American Psychological

Association to assist men to challenge what they term, 'some aspects of traditional masculinity…'

Defined as,

> 'encompassing a set of norms, ideas and beliefs about what it means to be a man. Such beliefs include identifying men as self reliant, emotionally reticent, focused on work over family and oversexed.'

In some cases, this rigid view of themselves is likely to result in men both perpetrating and experiencing violence.

Three of its recommendations include exploring the link between traditional forms of masculinity and the encouragement of aggressive behaviour in boys by family, peers and the media.

They encourage men's positive involvement in family life. We have moved on from what Lynne Segal describes as the typical family man of the 1950s whose commitment to the family consisted of

> 'DIY with hammers, saws, boring and drilling tools, screws, paint brushes.'[27]

But men still need to be more involved in the emotional side of things, not just because it would take some burden off their female partners but because they would gain emotional benefit themselves.

Their third recommendation is to seek help in healthcare. The numbers of male suicides in the UK is rising every year, and early intervention would clearly prevent at least some men taking their own lives.

Mask off: masculinity redefined by JJ Bola[28] is written for young, (preferably teenage) mainly male, readers. However, its clear, incisive, direct but unthreatening approach makes it a very useful book for anyone interested in challenging the damage caused by masculine stereotypes.

The author, JJ Bola describes himself as,

> 'a young Black, working-class, university educated straight man living in London.'

He goes on to say,

> 'I am privileged as a male'.

His main contention is that we can make choices about who and what we want to be. It will not always be easy but, he reminds us,

> 'Manhood, much like masculinity, is not a fixed entity. It is ever changing, it is fluid and more importantly, it is and can be anything you want it to be.'

JJ Bola writes about his own childhood growing up in North London in a Congolese community and,

> 'somewhere along the line I had transitioned into a man with a hard exterior, as did many of the boys I grew up with.'

He describes his own experience of realising that he is not happy with this identity and how he sets about changing it. In a section of his book entitled *Male privilege* he credits his understanding of feminism in helping him forge a new way of seeing himself.

> 'Not only do feminists want to create a more equal society for women, they have also fought for the rights of men. Feminism is actually beneficial for men as it seeks to heal men and remove the pressure that patriarchal society places on them.'

But ultimately, he places responsibility for change on men themselves.

'Men... must hold themselves and other men accountable for the ways in which they benefit from male privilege and actively work to change that ... men must work to change other men'

Fragility and Instability

A booklet published by the UN[29] suggests strategies for men to try to end violence against women. It covers what they call 'patriarchal masculinities',

> 'which are connected to the definition of power as domination and control, how men can support one another to deal with peer pressure and to critically reflect upon messages they are given about male sexuality.'

They urge men to work with women to understand the benefits to both men and women in curbing violent behaviour. To this end they encourage employing positive strategies rather than placing blame.

They stress that not all men are the same with similar belief systems. Multiple strategies are needed to explore dominant beliefs and behaviours. Men should meet together in a safe space, where they can ask questions without being judged.

With this encouraging advice, we now turn our attention to Institutes of Higher Education.

Policies and Procedures

Every university states the values which guide its policy and practice. The value statements typically emphasise equality, mutual respect, courtesy and dignified behaviour.

Manchester University, for instance, begins its Equality, Diversity and Inclusion Policy by stating that:

> 'The University is committed to promoting equality and promoting an environment where all members of its community are treated with respect and dignity.'

The introduction to Manchester's Dignity at Work and Study policy also insists that:

> 'All members of the University community, whether staff or students, are required to treat each other in a friendly, courteous and dignified manner. This requirement also applies to visitors and those otherwise associated with the University.'

This is typical of the opening sentences of many of the procedures which we have examined.

From preceding chapters it is clear that despite these statements of intent from every university approached by us, many are failing to comply with their own guidance.

We understand the difficulties of changing the prevailing culture in society, which inevitably affects attitudes in universities, but we feel that it has become imperative to challenge practices which discourage these well-intentioned policies and procedures from being effective.

Deeply entrenched attitudes, learned from an early age, are undoubtedly extremely hard to shift, but universities are perhaps uniquely placed to undertake such an initiative.

The fact that they are to a large extent closed communities leads to some of the often uncensored abuse we have written about, but this also gives them the opportunity to develop helpful strategies.

We have stated unequivocally that sanctions against sexual harassment and abuse should be employed and enforced to act as a signal of determination to put policies into effective practice and also to act as a deterrent. It is vital that all students and staff feel confident that these are not empty words.

However, it is indisputably preferable to prevent the need for such measures by instigating activities within university communities which help to deter abusive behaviour from taking place at all.

Universities can and should act as beacons of exemplary practice.

Universities are communities of young people and scholars. They are interdependent, each group relying on the other for their very existence. Trust is a vital ingredient for maintaining success in their relationship. Working together to create a productive climate is a necessary component.

We have an extraordinary recent example of the potency of collaborative action between young and old uniting against climate change. Fifteen-year-old Greta Thunberg, in tune with 90-year-old David Attenborough, have together alerted the world to the dangers we are facing if we do not act. Greta Thunberg has ignited a powerful reaction among young people in particular, but she has also galvanised older generations into demonstrating their concern.

In order to make a real and lasting difference to attitudes on the subject of sexual misconduct generally and sexual harassment and abuse in particular, the issue needs to be taken seriously.

A genuine desire to tackle sexual harassment and abuse in universities has got to come from both students and university staff.

We offer some strategies that can be tried, some already proven to be successful.

It is probable that young people are more likely to be swayed by hearing from members of their own generation. Student leaders have followers and our suggestion is that they should be called upon to bring these issues to the attention of their peers and to present ideas which might result in universities becoming safer places for all. There are some encouraging signs.

Consent Training

Obviously by the time they arrive at university, students will have been exposed to all sorts of experiences at home, at school and outside which will influence the way they view themselves and the world they live in. They will have formulated some personal moral values. Some, particularly older students, will have had sexual experiences, others will still be comparatively innocent. Most will probably have opinions on what constitutes sexual consent.

Because of this variety of experience, there is a great need to tell all students about the values of the university and the behaviour expected of students. So we are glad that students can use the internet to access workshops on consent training advertised by many universities. A selection includes Cambridge, Bristol, Sussex, SOAS, Edinburgh and Oxford. In the light of the current publicity about sexual abuse in universities it would be surprising if most universities were not offering this opportunity or planning to do so.

In August 2015, the NUS reported on an ambassador programme to train participants from 20 student unions in running consent workshops. These ambassadors then developed workshops which they went on to deliver to universities. Significantly they decided to target new students and sports society presidents.

The feedback from participants (120 men and 175 women) was that 91% agreed that they had taken away a better understanding of sexual consent from the workshops and that 87% would recommend the workshops to other students. An important by-product was that the Student Unions involved developed links to local organisations and services. At Sussex University the workshops were officially endorsed by the Sussex Men's Rugby and the Women's Football club. Tennis and other sports groups are now being trained to deliver the workshops to their clubs.

(In some universities we were told that that workshops were more successful when they were run by men.)

The workshops seem to be running successfully and in December 2018 the NUS published a consent workshop guide for use in all universities.

We have found several definitions of sexual consent but the simplest comes from an American Health Care institution:

> Sexual consent is an agreement to partake in sexual activity. Both people must agree to sex.[30]

That is the starting point. They go on to offer a simple mnemonic (FRIES) adopted by several British universities:

Sexual consent should be:

- Freely given
- Reversible
- Informed
- Enthusiastic
- Specific[31]

These easy-to-digest guidelines are taken up and explored by Louise, writing as an alumna of UCL.

Louise stresses the importance of *enthusiastic* sexual consent (both 'giving and getting'). She writes:

> (This) 'contributes to respectful, equal and fulfilling relationships. Any sexual activity that occurs without consent is against the law.'

She goes on to recommend sexual consent online training.

> 'Freedom to consent means doing something because you WANT TO.' (her capitals.)

She then gives examples of situations where choice is *not* given freely, including the use of coercion or force, blackmail through social images and, very important in our view

> 'where there is a power imbalance between two people due to age, status/position.'

Finally Louise writes

> 'consent is not ongoing – consent needs to be negotiated every time you have sex and during sex.'[32]

In some universities all Freshers will have to attend compulsory consent workshops from September 2019.

Oxford University has published a useful *Consent Workshop resource for facilitators* which is available to be accessed online.

Huffpost has published an article by Celia Hart, who started running consent workshops at Cambridge in 2015 in her role as Women's Officer. She lists.[33]

> '7 Things A University Sexual Consent Workshop Leader Wants You to Know'

- Sexual consent workshops are a response to a real problem.

    'During my time at university someone was accused of rape and went to trial. A girl wearing a short skirt is not responsible for being attacked.'

- Resistance from some staff:

    'They tried to fob me off with excuses about why it wasn't appropriate to run them.'

- Some students were worried that their parents would be alarmed about such workshops being run at the beginning of their first term.
- Consent workshops are not about attacking men. The workshops covered victim blaming, lad culture and male victims
- You have to make the workshop not feel like a lesson.

    'We sit round a table and discuss practical ways of telling people what is happening, or (when) you want something to stop'.

- They work much better when they are peer led – normally by students in the year above.

    'If someone is the same age as you, you're much more likely to listen than if they are the same age as your parents.'

- Sexual consent workshops should be given in schools.

    'The opinion forming stage of your life is much earlier.'[34]

It is worth applauding the strenuous efforts made by Warwick University, where instances of gross misogyny were outlined in a previous chapter. It serves as a useful example of the need to persevere in the face of strong reactions both for and against interventions.

In 2015, George Lawlor, a student at Warwick, gained notoriety by writing an article in *The Tab* (a National Student Newspaper) and also appeared on the Victoria Derbyshire Show complaining about an invitation to a consent workshop, which he took as an insult.

Warwick University rejected the complaint and in 2017 began to hold *I get consent* weeks at the university. Bystander intervention workshops were available across all faculties, accessible information about where to get help was made available, anonymous requests for information and help are answered by student volunteers.

An Independent Sexual Violence Advisor (ISVA) has an office in the Student Union, there is a very large wellbeing team on site and a walk-in centre where students are seen within 15–20 minutes.

A student liaison officer guides both the reporter (complainant) and the respondent (accused) throughout any process.

Workshops Alone Are Not Enough

Although she strongly encourages workshops and bystander training, Lilia Giugni, CEO and Co-founder of Genpol, an organisation carrying out research, advocacy and consultancy on gender, warned us that on their own they are not effective unless there is visible serious commitment from the university senior managers.

This view was echoed by many of our interviewees. As one senior manager explained to us

> "leadership at the top has to be committed if there are to be any lasting improvements."

And when the Vice Chancellors and other senior people are committed, things can change quite quickly.

Helena Kennedy QC, human rights lawyer, was Principal of Mansfield College in Oxford. She told us of her efforts to get things moving.

> "I was asked to lead a working Party at Oxford on this (sexual abuse). It became clear to me that there was too much amateurism about the handling of these issues by colleges. Oxford is complex because it has over thirty colleges and each claims its own sovereignty in dealing with complaints and grievances. Disciplinary matters are often dealt with internally and I am afraid not always well. The temptation to protect a college's reputation has in the past outstripped concerns about the victim. However, I found a real willingness amongst a new cadre of Heads of House to get this all sorted. It is vital that there is a professional entity independent of colleges available to deal with such complaints. This was in my Report and was agreed."

Other universities which are finding ways to prevent abuse or deal with incidents when they arise are:

The University of Birmingham which makes reporting easy.

University of York is one of the universities which gives names of the staff trained to receive reports.

Cardiff University has a very good schedule of places where support can be found, both inside and outside the university, and

Staffordshire University has a sexual violence support team which is pictured on their website with the promise that they will offer continuing support through any procedure.

A senior lecturer also told us that at Newcastle University

> "student wellbeing is really well catered for. The response to distress is good and there is a separate wellbeing office which is very good and well publicised."

Bystander Intervention

Begun in the US, Bystander Intervention workshops are now being run in British Universities. The basic concept is to equip men or women with the skills

> 'to interrupt behaviour to prevent sexual violence'.

In universities, this usually signifies intervening when inappropriate or unwanted behaviour is witnessed.

Professor Alison Phipps of Sussex University said to us:

> "Bystander intervention is seen as less threatening to men than other strategies."

Good training is required to give confidence to the participants, most often student volunteers, who have to make a decision about intervening to prevent misconduct by one of their peers, usually at social events.

This can lead to a tricky situation if the Bystander finds themselves in a position where the miscreant has consumed a lot of alcohol or is much bigger than them. It can consist of a friendly word of warning, turning off the lights or switching off the music. The main point is that they should not ignore a potentially unpleasant encounter.

A professor of law and gender equality told us that bystander training has the advantage of involving men in taking responsibility for influencing the behaviour of other men. There is a value in:

> "Young men calling out other young men."

In 2016 Public Health England published a review of the evidence for Bystander Intervention and their conclusions were positive. They noted a decreased perpetration of violence, increased knowledge about violence, decreased sexist attitudes (including peer sexist attitudes), decreased denial of violence as a problem and increased confidence to intervene.

The Goodlad Initiative

An approach which seems to be successful in reaching and persuading men to reflect on their motives and actions is *The Goodlad Initiative*. Workshops are pioneered and run by Dan Guinness and his team.

Dan Guinness is a former professional rugby player. Since we have repeatedly been informed that much of the abusive behaviour in universities appears to emanate from sports teams, and rugby clubs in particular, this presumably aids his credibility when working with men who may otherwise express scepticism.

He told us that their workshops,

> "give men an open space to have necessary conversations and ask difficult questions of themselves.
>
> They allow men to resist conformity to the negative aspects of masculinity."

The workshops are founded upon the question:

> 'Who do you really want to be?'

Dan stressed the point that the sessions are not run as a lecture, nor are the men made to feel that they are put on trial.

What he called a Theory of Change involves giving the participants time to constantly engage and re-engage emotionally with each of the issues raised.

When discussing consent in sexual relationships, the message is straightforward: we need to shift away from,

> 'This is what I want. Do you consent?' to 'What do you want?'

This tribute from an Oxford university team rugby player suggests that these methods obtain results.

> "I have certainly seen a big attitude shift in the sports teams since I've been here... And I'm sure the the Goodlad Initiative workshops are responsible for that improvement."

Working in Schools

Several people who spoke to us felt that training on this subject needs to start long before young people arrive at university.

As Pierre Hallien, a final year student at Oxford University, said to us:

> "I feel that education on what is meant by consent in sexual relationships needs to begin much earlier.
> People as young as fourteen start going to parties to get drunk, so it seems a bit ridiculous that training on this subject seems to consist of an hour when they start university."

The Goodlad workshops are also run in secondary schools, where they are designed for boys aged 12–17 years and their teachers.

> "This age group is most susceptible to the opinions of their peers", Dan told us, "but the social norms surrounding them have not yet been solidified."

Attitudes may be formed even younger, as John Swain found.

John Swain spent two months observing and talking to a group of year six boys in a state junior school.[35] His thesis is that

> 'boys use football as a way of constantly negotiating and performing their masculinity.'

These boys were very good footballers and they not only excluded girls along with boys who were considered 'feminised' (sic) by their lack of sporting skills, but subjected them to homophobic abuse. In playing football for literally thousands of hours, the boys were 'practising to become men'. John Swain describes football, even for boys as young as this, as

> 'full of aggressive intent, about winners and losers, territorial, occupying space through domination... Football games provide an open stage for the boys to perform their masculinities on a regular basis... scenes of highly visible, ritualised and stylised exhibitions.'

As well as demonstrating excellence on the football field, the boys in question are referred to as 'highly intelligent, high achievers, able to tell a good joke...' Other boys saw themselves as altogether subordinate on the basis of their lack of footballing proficiency.

It is of course possible, as they progress through secondary school, that the boys in this group will meet others who play even better, or learn to respect differences among their peers but, sadly, the behaviour that Swain found is probably replicated in many primary schools across the country. Allowing young boys to adopt these attitudes at an early age (with the acquiescence of the other boys and the girls) does not augur well for their subsequent behaviour, should they choose to go to university.

Reading Fiction

Reading fiction can be an easier way into thinking about issues to do with gender and masculinity, than simply confronting young people with opprobrium.

Bill's New Frock by Anne Fine,[36] aimed at 7/8-year-olds, describes Bill's day at school when his mother dresses him in a frilly pink dress and he goes to school as a girl. From the outset he realises how different life is for a girl. Arriving late he is not told off but ushered into his classroom with soothing words. When the class reads Rapunzel he is delighted to be given the main character's role but finds that all he has to say very intermittently is 'ooh'. At lunchtime he is ready to kick a ball about but instead goes to the library to read comics. He is not allowed to get his clothes dirty. He is uncomfortable and bored.

The audience for Gene Kemp's *The Turbulent Term of Tyke Tiler*[37] is 11/12-year-olds. Tyke and his friend Danny Price are constantly getting into scrapes and into trouble at school. Finally Tyke saves the day when a serious problem arises and Tyke is eventually greeted as a hero by classmates. It is only on the very last page that Tyke is revealed to be a girl. Having read Tyke Tiler with many young students, I (Eva) can testify to the outrage when this is discovered, particularly by the boys.

'He can't be a girl!'

Why not?

> 'Because he is strong and gets into trouble all the time and plays football...'

Books like these challenge preconceptions without directly confronting boys and girls but they allow them to ponder on their own prejudices.

Challenging Prevailing Attitudes

Ultimately the ideal scenario is for men and women to work together to gradually change current notions of toxic masculinity and feeble females. The psychologist Carol Dweck at Stanford University has been conducting significant experiments to persuade us to take a less rigid view or 'mindset' on the permanent nature of ability.[38] Her theory is that when people fall apart if challenged, they are succumbing to a 'learned helplessness' that hinders them from making any progress. Failure she says can be interpreted in different ways; we can use failure to validate our static view of ourselves or we can use failure as a way of 'growing our abilities.' She calls this having *fixed* or *malleable* attributes. To help us make this mental adjustment, we all need to switch to believing in the plasticity of the brain as advocated by the neuroscientist, Susan Greenfield[39]. Carol Dweck clearly demonstrates that,

> 'the human brain has the ability to adapt to its surroundings.'[40]

We do not have to take what we are given. Exposed to the right environment and experiences we can change even deeply held attitudes.

As long ago as 1955, George Kelly published his seminal book *A Theory of Personality: the psychology of personal constructs*.[41]

Kelly's theory is that people develop personal constructs about the way the world works. They then use these constructs to make sense of their experiences and also to make predictions about what will happen in the future and how they will deal with events. But past experiences need not dictate our reactions. Every individual has the capacity to interpret and evaluate what is happening to them. They can take a leap into the unknown, with the 'risk of living with a certain amount of confusion' to try new responses.

> 'It is not so much what a man (sic) is that counts as it is what he continues to make of himself.'[42]

It is our contention that Carol Dweck's experiments and Kelly's theory give us hope that both women and men can challenge stereotypes, make their own decisions about how they view the world and adjust their behaviour accordingly. Men can summon up the courage to defy expected norms of masculinity and women can feel safer to express their desires.

A senior lecturer told us:

> "You need tenacity to keep fighting."

And, as Julia Buckingham, President of UUK said to us:

> "We need to keep the conversation going."

8

Ending the Abuse

Unless they improve their performance in tackling sexual harassment and abuse, universities will suffer further damage to their reputation. Pressure from media reports will increase and political criticism will become sharper. If universities cannot persuade politicians and the public that they have a grip on the problem, it seems inevitable that demands will be made for direct action by government. An increase in regulation may not be the best way to reduce sexual abuse in universities but it will certainly prove uncomfortable for Vice Chancellors and senior managers.

To tackle the problem effectively, a major programme of reform is necessary. Unfortunately, most universities seem in no mood to institute substantial change. They should have responded to the turnaround in the public attitude to sexual harassment and abuse by reviewing their performance and adopting better policies but many have not. The unhappy truth which emerges from our research is that the issue is still given too little attention by senior management, the necessary information is not collected and most universities have still not equipped themselves with the required expertise. Our Freedom of Information Requests showed that only 9 out of 102 universities in England and Wales are carrying out a substantial programme of reform. None of this suggests that a moment of epiphany is very near.

Unless universities change direction, the next decade will probably resemble the last. Many universities will remain amateurish in their practices and frequently on the defensive as more scandals are uncovered. Ministers will express concern and experts will call for thorough-going action. Universities might make a few gestures in response to criticism but, on the basis of their performance so far, many will do little more.

Most depressing of all is the effect on the people who work and study in universities. Each year produces a new cohort of victims who will suffer the misery of sexual harassment, abuse and assault. University careers will be blighted and the damage to self-esteem, to self-confidence and to the victims' ability to form trusting and fulfilling relationships is likely, from the evidence we have heard, to persist throughout much of their adult life. As one victim told us:

> "It happened a long time ago but I still cannot put it behind me."

With so many people at risk, more of the same cannot be acceptable. Universities must do better than this.

Motivation

Faced with this continuing disaster, it is tempting to draft a model programme of reform for universities to implement. It is an easy document to write. During our research we compiled a checklist of over 20 actions which universities should take to reduce sexual harassment and abuse. For completeness, we include the list as an Appendix to this chapter. Each proposal is worthwhile and, if all these proposals were enacted with enthusiasm and commitment, universities would become much safer for students and for staff.

Unfortunately what is lacking is not prescription but motivation. Most universities apparently do not believe that they need to change course and adopt different policies. Both of us have learnt during our long working lives that prescribing policy statements and action plans when senior managers are not really listening is a waste of energy and might even prove to be counterproductive. We are both familiar with situations where, once a few boxes have been ticked, the documents are set aside to gather dust in some forgotten file or to languish unread in some unflagged electronic folder. Frequently, all that remains is the complacent and damaging impression that the problem has been addressed and dealt with.

Outside pressure might be useful and, if universities prove intransigent, might even be essential. We deal with that possibility in the next chapter. But this would represent a serious failure of will and process. Surely universities have the capacity to reduce and perhaps eliminate this appalling problem by the application of their own good sense and determination. However, before this can to be accomplished, all Vice Chancellors will have to be persuaded that current policies are not working and that substantial reform is essential.

An Authoritative Survey

Given goodwill, an opportunity to open a debate about future policy and practice is readily available. It is a truism in management circles that, before attempting to solve a problem, it is necessary to understand its extent, severity and nature. Unfortunately, universities have not taken this preliminary step. In Chapter 1 we noted, with great surprise, that there is a dearth of good quality data about every aspect of sexual harassment and abuse.

Universities are meant to believe in rigorous research and evidence-based decision-making. So it is extraordinary that universities have adopted policies and procedures which affect the life chances of so many students and staff without collecting the basic evidence and without undertaking the necessary research.

Guesswork is not good enough. Unless universities collect the necessary data, their efforts are likely to be ill-directed, resources will be wasted and programmes will fail. We have been told of many occasions when these mistakes have been made.

The public interest case is also very strong. Students, staff, the general public and the government are entitled to know whether universities are being managed in a manner which provides a safe space to study and work.

Viewed objectively, the case for an authoritative survey is unanswerable. The higher education sector, either directly or through Universities UK (UUK) and the other major organisations which represent universities,[1] should commission a representative survey to collect information about the extent and nature of sexual harassment and abuse in British universities. As we noted in Chapter 1, the survey is easily affordable. UUK might not have sufficient funds, but the university sector as a whole certainly has. Based on the Australian experience we have estimated that such a survey would cost each university an average of about £2,000.

The way the survey is conducted is important. In the first place it should be undertaken independently. There is a great deal of suspicion in the university community already and it would be disastrous if the survey was organised in-house and be subject to the allegation that the results could be manipulated. Second, the survey must be undertaken by a professional organisation experienced in such work. The results must be fully representative of the students and staff in higher education and this is no task for an amateur, however well-meaning. Third, it should be stressed that what is required are authoritative national statistics. Just as we have resisted the temptation to name and shame individual universities, so the survey should not be designed to draw up some league table showing the number of incidents by each university.

That approach would produce an atmosphere of bitter competition between universities when what is needed is a cooperative effort to make improvements across the whole sector.

Much is riding on this decision. A good survey would sweep away the myths and speculation and reveal the truth about the extent and nature of sexual harassment and abuse in universities. It would signal the beginning of professionalism, with policy being based on evidence rather than on untested assumptions. It would also help to restore a belief in the determination of universities to reduce sexual misconduct.

The present situation cannot be defended. Universities need to honour their reputation as centres of learning, collect the necessary information and replace guesswork with knowledge.

Detachment

Many of the people we interviewed referred to the gulf of understanding between victims who had suffered sexual harassment or abuse and the administrators and managers who have the responsibility for dealing with the problem. Some victims are very bitter:

> "They just did not seem to care about what happened to me."

One Student Union representative told us that she had been trying for many months to persuade the Dean that sexual harassment was taking place regularly at university social events and that this abuse should be dealt with. The Dean listened politely but did nothing. Eventually after a particularly unpleasant episode of sexual harassment, she went to see him and her sense of frustration became so overwhelming that she broke down in tears. The effect on the Dean was startling.

> "For the first time he realised that this was important to me and ought to be important to him."

The Dean called in a female tutor. She was sympathetic and helpful. She acted as an interpreter, describing to the Dean the disrespect and harassment which women in the university regularly experienced at social events and explaining why the Student Union representative felt that the university was failing in its responsibilities. This was a key moment and things gradually began to change.

What impressed us in this account is not that the Student Union Rep burst into tears, which she found desperately embarrassing, but the fact that, until the show of emotion, the Dean was so detached, as if sexual harassment was just one of the many inconsequential things which students complain about.

This air of detachment is also apparent in many of the procedures which we examined in Chapter 5. Universities say that they want victims to report incidents of sexual harassment and abuse. When a complainant comes forward, s/he is entitled to sympathetic support not only from the people s/he talks to about her/his ordeal but also in the wording of the procedure documents which set out how her/his complaint will be dealt with. Unfortunately it is very rare for the procedure documents to offer words of comfort and reassurance. In most instances, what greets a vulnerable complainant is not warmth and understanding but strict rules, cold legal language and an insistence that an arcane process should be followed.

This sense of detachment is obviously inappropriate. Victims are suffering distress and the university owes a duty of care to its students and staff. At first, we found it difficult to understand why the attitude of senior managers and the tone of the procedures are not infused with sympathy and concern.

Familiarisation with the processes began to produce an explanation. We came to realise that many senior managers had never actually talked to a victim of sexual harassment and abuse. Investigations are usually carried out by middle managers; senior managers rarely hear about an incident of sexual harassment and abuse from the lips of a victim. Almost everything they learn about sexual harassment and abuse is second hand.

No doubt some senior managers will insist that they are fully aware of the seriousness of the incidents which prompt complaints of sexual harassment or abuse. However there is an important difference between reading or being told about an incident and seeing and listening to a victim.

Before we began our interviews, both of us had read widely about sexual harassment and abuse. We might have imagined that the meetings with victims would produce few surprises. We were utterly wrong. The interviews affected us deeply. When a victim describes what happened, s/he re-lives the incident. You see the outrage, the pain and the fear. S/he attempts to explain the difficulty of coming to terms with what occurred. Should s/he tell family and friends or try to keep it a secret? Victims suffer a loss of confidence in their own judgement: they have difficulty trusting friends and colleagues. Many victim/survivors told us of the terrible fear that they might come face to face with the perpetrator. Although the feeling is unwarranted, they also carry a burden of guilt. Their distress is palpable. No one will have a clear idea of the misery caused by sexual harassment and abuse until they meet the victims.

Direct Experience

Involvement must replace detachment. No one in universities should decide policy on sexual harassment and abuse until they have had direct experience of the suffering of the victims. As we described in Chapter 2, we were told about a conference of senior managers where two brave women described their abuse and its effects. In the subsequent discussion, it became clear that many of the managers had never previously heard victims talk about these awful experiences. The session made a strong impression. One manager admitted:

> 'I don't think I understood properly before I heard the details of how these poor women had suffered.'

The key person in determining the priority given to sexual harassment and abuse in any university is, of course, the Vice Chancellor. The Vice Chancellor's attitude to sexual harassment and abuse is overwhelmingly important in deciding whether a university commits itself to fundamental reform or continues with the old ways. People in the university community understand this very well. One academic we interviewed described the responsibility of the Vice Chancellor in graphic terms.

> "As a mother I want to know that the Vice Chancellor of the university my daughter is attending has strong feelings about sexual abuse and intends to do something about it."

Some of the people we interviewed had come to the conclusion that the best way to secure the support of the Vice Chancellor is to make sure that s/he knows about sexual abuse at first hand.

We were very impressed by the initiative taken by the Student Union in one Midlands university. The President of the Student Union asked the incoming Vice Chancellor to meet a group of victims of sexual abuse and assault. He agreed and the Student Union arranged the meeting where 15 victim/survivors told their individual stories. They sat around the large table and the first victim/survivor began, bluntly and clearly

'Hi my name is ... and I was raped last year.'

The briefing continued until all the victim/survivors had spoken.

The meeting had a strong impact. The victim/survivors were impressed by how carefully the Vice Chancellor listened. He not only expressed sympathy but also promised changes. Better information is now available about the action to be taken after an incident and he gave a commitment to better funding for training.

The meeting also boosted the morale of the victim/survivors. The President of the Student Union told us that after the meeting one of the women said to her,

> "Before I was assaulted I was a feminist who stood up for myself. Afterwards I lost who I was and hid. Now I'm trying to be the person I used to be."

We strongly recommend that the Student Union in every university takes that initiative as a model and asks the Vice Chancellor to meet a group of students who have suffered sexual harassment and abuse. The meeting should not be regarded as an opportunity to make high profile speeches. The intention should be to ensure sure that the Vice Chancellor has direct experience of the suffering of victims and understands how difficult it is to survive sexual harassment and abuse. We believe that, if such meetings were to take place across the country, a substantial change will take place in the attitude of universities. After hearing directly from victim/survivors, we believe that Vice Chancellors are likely to give a higher priority to developing policies and procedures which deal effectively with this deplorable problem.

To ensure that the importance of this initiative is recognised, we propose that it should be formally supported by Student Unions, by the NUS but also by organisations which represent universities, including UUK, MillionPlus and the GuildHE.

Reform of the Procedures

During our examination of the documents sent to us in response to our FOI requests, we found many reasons for universities to review and improve their procedures. Duplication and overlaps need to be removed, signposts should be included so that it is obvious which procedure will be used for each issue and the procedures should be written in language which is easily understood. However this wide-ranging reform, although essential, goes beyond the scope of this book. We therefore focus only on those procedures which deal with sexual harassment and abuse.

The great majority of universities do not have a specially designed procedure to address complaints of sexual harassment and abuse. As we explained in Chapter 5, many universities deal with sexual complaints within general complaints procedures which deal with many diverse issues. Typically, there will be a list of between six and twenty examples of matters where complaints might arise. Sexual harassment, abuse and assault might be referred to once or twice in the list, alongside issues as diverse as, for instance, rowdy behaviour and inaccuracies in university supplied materials. All complaints, of whatever nature, are then taken through the same procedure.

An alternative approach, used by some universities, is to deal with complaints of sexual harassment and abuse within procedures which are called 'Anti-Harassment and Bullying' or 'Dignity and Respect'. At first sight this approach appears more promising: the impression is given that the university has a procedure which is more focused on sexual misconduct. Unfortunately this is often an illusion. On closer inspection many of these procedures are non-specific and have been written to deal with a variety of issues, often including non-sexual bullying, discrimination and victimisation on grounds of race, religion, sexuality and disability.

This is the wrong approach. The notion that complaints of sexual harassment and abuse should be dealt with in the same way as complaints about very different issues fails to recognise the particular nature of sexual harassment and abuse and disregards the very specific needs of victims.

Needs of Victims

The case against using the normal complaints procedure to handle complaints of sexual harassment and abuse is best demonstrated by listing the problems which arise when a generic complaints procedure is used.

The first difficulty concerns the time restrictions which limit access to the complaints procedures. Like other researchers, we found that victims/survivors of sexual harassment and abuse need time to come to terms with their ordeal. Sometimes it takes victims many weeks and months before they can even think about reporting the incident. So declaring that only recent incidents may be reported, as many universities choose to do, is inappropriate. It denies justice to the victim and deprives universities of vital information about the prevalence and nature of sexual misconduct in their institution.

Victim/survivors of sexual harassment and abuse need very particular advice and support. Once they decide to report, they need those services to be made available very quickly. Care and sympathy need to be provided by people who understand the traumatic effects of abuse. This is not a job for well-meaning but inexperienced all-rounders. Such vital services are best offered as part of a specifically designed procedure which ensures that the first contact with the complainant is handled by a properly trained specialist.

The standard three-stage general complaints procedure which we described in Chapter 5 contains complex language, much legalese and frequent references to other policies and procedures. We were told by our interviewees that these procedures are very off-putting. Complaints of sexual harassment and abuse are made by victims who are struggling to cope with the aftermath of an ordeal which has caused them great anguish. The procedure must be accessible and easily understood. Moreover, the tone of the procedure should be warm and sympathetic rather than cold and challenging.

The general complaints procedures also tend to include features which victims of sexual harassment and abuse find frightening and insulting. As we explained in Chapter 5, the first stage in the standard procedure asks the complainant to approach the person against whom the complaint is made in an attempt to achieve some resolution. This might be sensible if the complaint is about some routine matter like the use of laboratory equipment, but to even suggest that an alleged victim of sexual abuse should go and see the alleged perpetrator is outrageous. Many of the victim/survivors whom we interviewed were greatly upset by such a proposal. It has no place in a procedure for dealing with complaints of sexual harassment and abuse.

Most complaints procedures suggest that, to aid resolution, a process of mediation should be offered to the complainant. Every victim/survivor we interviewed told us that they never wanted to see the alleged perpetrator again. To suggest that they go to see a mediator in company with the perpetrator is completely inappropriate.

General complaints procedures, including 'Anti-Harassment and Bullying' and 'Dignity and Respect' procedures, invariably include a very heavy warning against making false accusations. Complainants are told that a false accusation is likely to lead to disciplinary action. So a victim, who is already in two minds about making a complaint, gains the impression that, if the alleged perpetrator denies the offence and is believed, it might be the complainant who is punished.

This provision might be appropriate in respect of other offences but to issue that warning to complainants in a procedure concerning sexual harassment and abuse is insensitive and damaging. The pressing problem faced by universities is not the tiny number of false accusations but the under-reporting of sexual assaults which are taking place but never recorded. To threaten complainants with the possibility of disciplinary action has the opposite effect to the one which universities say they want: instead of encouraging reporting, it acts as a significant deterrent.

A Well-designed Procedure

Theoretically it would be possible to amend the existing procedures to make it clear that inappropriate clauses are to be disregarded in cases of sexual harassment and abuse. But this would make the existing procedures even more cumbersome and confusing. A much better solution is to extract sexual harassment and abuse cases from the generic procedures and to design a special procedure which takes proper account of the nature of sexual abuse and the specific needs of the victims.

Fortunately this is not a new idea. We have identified 27 universities which have introduced something amounting to a specially designed procedure for cases of sexual harassment and abuse.

A few universities have made a significant improvement. The procedure introduced by Goldsmiths University, for instance, is complete in itself without requiring reference to other documents. Advice and support are detailed and the language is easy to understand. The procedure used by Keele and the new procedure introduced by Warwick also have much to recommend them.

Other universities have made more modest changes. Eleven universities apply the new procedures only to student complaints and not to staff. More seriously, some of the new procedures also contain unhelpful clauses which have been carried over from the old-style generic procedures.

Nevertheless, although 27 universities represent only a small proportion of the universities in England and Wales and although some of the new procedures require further amendment, the introduction of specific procedures for sexual harassment and abuse represents a significant step forward and should be adopted by all universities. Naturally the changeover should be properly planned. We were discouraged to learn of the problems which arose in Cambridge when a new procedure was introduced. A different definition of harassment led the university to set aside some complaints which had been lodged before the change. Complainants felt angry and abandoned. We trust that this decision will be reversed.[2]

The unfortunate events in Cambridge reinforce the need to place care for the complainant at the heart of each new procedure. The presumption must be that a complainant, by reporting an incident of alleged sexual abuse, is helping the university. Until and unless an investigation proves otherwise, a complainant is entitled to be believed. S/he should be afforded good quality advice and support by well-trained university staff. And it should be accepted that, having submitted a complaint, the complainant remains part of the process until a final decision is reached.

Proper rights for complainants should be spelled out. Complainants should, for instance, have the right to be heard by the disciplinary panel which is considering the case against the alleged perpetrator. They should be guaranteed the right to receive progress reports on the case and they should receive notification of the outcome at the same time as the accused. More controversially, the complainant should have a right of appeal against the decision of the disciplinary panel which has adjudicated on her/his complaint.

As we explained in Chapter 5, the complainant's reputation is at stake in the hearing. Allowing the accused the right of appeal against the decision of the disciplinary panel, while ignoring any concerns expressed by the complainant, is unbalanced and unjust. We were therefore delighted to learn that Warwick University has responded to the problems which they experienced in 2018 and 2019 by introducing the right of appeal for complainants. This is a very constructive development and is strongly recommended to all universities. It brings a new element of fairness to the procedures and helps to combat the widely held view that universities are more concerned to help alleged perpetrators than to support victims.

A More Sympathetic Tone

Introducing a new complaints procedure for sexual harassment and abuse also provides the opportunity for a much needed change of tone. Cold legalese and impersonal prose, in which the victim is always referred to in the third person, are best avoided. There is no reason why the procedure cannot address the victim directly in a conversational and supportive manner. St John's College, Oxford, manages to do this without compromising the impartiality which it must demonstrate when investigating a complaint. An early part of the procedure reads as follows:

'If you think you are being harassed the College strongly encourages you to do something about it. This section of the guidance sets out information on the help available to you. There are also flowcharts available to guide you visually through this process. The College recommends that you should discuss the situation with a harassment adviser before taking any other steps in response to the alleged harassment. All College harassment advisers have received training to equip them to help you. Talking through the events and your feelings with the adviser will help you decide on the best way to deal with the behaviour and will clarify the options available to you.'

As well as sympathetic treatment, every complainant wants the issue to be dealt with speedily. That should be guaranteed in the new procedure. Given the right level of priority, we believe that a complaint of sexual harassment or abuse could be heard, investigated and a decision reached within a calendar month.

Universities have much to gain from these changes. A better designed and specific procedure which guarantees new rights to complainants will help to demonstrate that the university takes sexual harassment and abuse very seriously. The reforms would be another constructive move in the necessary task of restoring the credibility of university processes and reducing the cynicism which we found to be very common in the university community.

Culture Change

A member of the Governing body of a London University told us, rather sadly, that although he was confident that his university would eventually reduce sexual misconduct, he was much less optimistic about changing the unpleasant culture which fuels that misconduct.[3] He went on to quote the American management guru, Peter Drucker, who argued that, if there is a conflict between the strategy of an organisation and its culture, the culture always wins. In Drucker's words,

> 'Culture eats strategy for breakfast.'

In earlier chapters we quoted two senior managers who told us that, because sexual harassment and abuse is common in British society, it is inevitable that universities would have the same problem. Although this is obviously true, we argued earlier that this mind-set can encourage a feeling that there is little prospect of any substantial improvement in universities until British culture changes. We regard that conclusion as too pessimistic. Universities need not follow the national trend; they should strive to set their own.

In Chapter 7, we suggested that a culture of sexual harassment and abuse is sustained by an aggressive notion of masculinity and by an outdated stereotype of womanhood. We accept that these attitudes are deep-rooted and difficult to eliminate. However, the impetus for change has to start somewhere and, as universities have a stated commitment to equality, dignity and respect, it seems appropriate that they should act as leaders in seeking to change our culture so that these laudable qualities become the basis of all private and public relationships.

Of course, universities cannot shut out the distorted and damaging values which are still current in the outside world, but they do have particular opportunities. To some extent universities are closed communities, making their own rules and applying their own discipline. They also have unique access to young people who will determine the nature of British society in the coming decades. Universities can create indelible impressions on the lives of their students, for good or ill. Change in academe should act as a catalyst for change in the rest of Britain.

In Chapter 7 we described some encouraging developments. Workshops which explore the nature of consent are becoming a normal part of the first term in university. More universities are training volunteers to be Bystanders, who watch out for situations when sexual abuse might occur and intervene to reduce the danger. Some universities are encouraging student leaders to act as advocates for the values of dignity and respect.

That is the good news and some of it is very good. Unfortunately too few universities are following the example of the best. There is still a widespread impression that trying to change the sexual culture of universities is just a marginal activity – underfunded, under-regarded and relying on the enthusiasm of Student Unions and the goodwill of a few staff. Some universities have moved these activities centre-stage, but elsewhere culture change initiatives seem like so much of the universities' approach to sexual harassment and abuse: rather amateurish and with little active support from the top.

The best approach would be for the less successful to learn from the experience of the most committed and act accordingly. Unfortunately, in spite of the efforts of UUK and others, universities seem to find it difficult to learn from each other. As in much else, success seems to depend heavily on the active support and leadership of each Vice Chancellor. Therefore the first step towards creating a university culture which is more equal, humane and respectful is for the Vice Chancellor and the university Governing Body to declare publicly and unequivocally that they intend to develop a programme to transform the sexual culture of their institution.

Collaborative

The university community is not easily captivated by warm words. Both staff and students will need to be convinced that the policy is for real and not just part of some Public Relations puff. The backing of the Student Unions and the trade unions will be essential and they should be reassured that the university will devote funds and people to the endeavour. To achieve credibility, the transformation programme must have the right level of prestige. The Vice Chancellor must be seen to be closely involved. A well-regarded manager should be given overall responsibility. Appropriately trained individuals should support representatives of the Student Union in delivering consent training. Volunteers who are recruited to assist should be accorded proper status. Achieving the position of a Bystander should be regarded as something to put on the CV – an accolade and not a chore.

The approach should be collaborative, gathering the participation of groups throughout the institution. Clubs, including sports clubs, play an important part in the life of a university. Determined efforts should be made to gain their active support and to persuade them to operate in accordance with the core values of equality, dignity and respect.

This approach will not be universally popular. Research by Alison Phipps and Isobel Young has shown some sports clubs, in particular, are the source of 'laddist' behaviour and even abuse.[4]

To eradicate these unpleasant tendencies, the support of club officers is crucial. They have authority and a measure of celebrity. Alongside other leaders of university opinion, they should be encouraged to act as advocates for the transformation programme. To emphasise the important leadership role of the clubs, each university should endorse a symbolic restriction: anyone whose behaviour is inconsistent with the values of the programme should not be eligible to be a club officer.

A good programme will make sure that each element not only has its own specific purpose but also sparks other initiatives. The

Bystanders should be regarded as part of a network, meeting to share experiences and to put forward recommendations to make the campus safer. The workshops can be used not only to explain the philosophy of consent but also to identify areas of difficulty and incomprehension. The knowledge gained by the trainers should be used to improve the courses and, if necessary, to develop others. To be successful, the transformation programme cannot be static. It must spawn ideas for further improvements.

Of course, changing the culture is not just about modifying behaviour, important as that is. At some point those deeply embedded notions of aggressive masculinity and submissive womanhood will have to be confronted, not just obliquely but directly.

There is a plethora of feminist research dismantling outdated female stereotypes and, in the last few years, there has been a resurgence of male studies into masculinity. The task faced by university reformers is how to stimulate interest in these issues on campus, not just among discrete and self-selecting groups but amongst the wider university community.

We note with regret that the nature of masculinity is rarely debated by men and almost never discussed between the sexes. Aspects of womanhood are more often discussed by women but, once again, those discussions rarely involve men. A determined attempt to change the culture of universities involves putting that right. We badly need a definition of modern masculinity and womanhood which is more fluid in its boundaries, more equal and respectful in its outcomes and which makes sense to people, however they define their sexuality.

That search would take us beyond the scope of this book. Therefore we recommend just two initiatives.

In Chapter 7 we applauded the work of Dan Guinness and his colleagues in designing the Goodlad Initiative. Every university would do well to use that project to stimulate an examination of male behaviour amongst their students and staff.

Second, universities should find a way to use the scholarship and knowledge of academics on their campus to bring the conclusions from recent research on masculinity and womanhood to the attention of everyone in their community. The findings will almost certainly be contested and that controversy can be used to stimulate much-needed debate.

Sex with Students

A programme to reduce sexual harassment and abuse is most likely to be successful if there is coherence in the university's approach, with each policy acting to reinforce the rest. Unfortunately there is one policy, common throughout the sector, which we regard as totally misjudged. It gives a message that is seriously at odds with university values and their declared objectives.

In Chapter 5 we revealed that 96 out of 102 universities in England and Wales permit teaching staff to have sex with their students. Although over half of the universities discourage such behaviour and require staff to report this sexual activity to their manager, they seem to take no action to prevent such relationships. Even more worrying, 46 universities give staff no explicit guidance on the matter. They do not even make a statement discouraging sex between staff and students – they say next to nothing on the subject and just watch it happen.

When we discussed this permissive attitude with people in the university community, we were surprised to find that many managers do not seem to have given much thought to the damage that this policy is causing.

When asked why all universities do not prohibit all teaching staff from having sex with their students, managers who support the status quo deploy four arguments against a prohibition.

- It is wrong in principle for a university to become involved in the private lives of its staff and students.
- Students are adults and are entitled to make their own decisions about sexual behaviour.
- A ban on sex is unenforceable and would drive such relationships underground.
- There are so many special circumstances – like pre-existing relationships and the difficulty of defining a 'student' when some postgraduate students also teach – that it would be virtually impossible to frame a prohibition which is both fair and workable.

There is, of course, some substance in these arguments. However, universities should balance the weight of these objections against the considerable harm caused by sexual relationships between members of staff and students. Our own examination has convinced us that the current permissive policy needs to be changed and that a ban should be introduced.

Our case for prohibition starts with an endorsement of the values which all universities declare in their policies and procedures. These documents emphasise the need for university staff to behave in an exemplary manner. One typical Dignity at Work policy states that:

> 'The student/teacher relationship is one of special trust. Teaching staff are required to recognise their professional and ethical responsibilities to protect the interests

of students, to respect the trust involved in the staff/
student relationship and to accept the obligations
inherent in that responsibility.'

No one reading that clause could reasonably imagine that these high standards of trust, professionalism and an ethical responsibility to protect students' interests could conceivably be met by a teacher who is having sex with one of their students. A serious contradiction exists between university policy and practice.

There is little to be admired in the behaviour of a member of staff who sleeps with a student but we are much less concerned with personal morality than with the resulting damage. People we interviewed told us that almost every such relationship ends by hurting the student. It also disrupts the smooth running of courses, feeds a suspicion of favouritism which weakens faith in the assessment process and leaves a residue of disharmony and cynicism which persists well beyond the end of the affair. Senior managers lose credibility for allowing the problem to develop and the reputation of the university is inevitably undermined.

Power and Vulnerability

Although students are adults in law, they often attend a university far away from family and close friends and feel isolated in the demanding environment of a university campus. Assistance and sympathetic support from academics and senior staff will be eagerly welcomed and can enhance the university experience for many students. But there is a dark side. Lonely and insecure students are vulnerable to grooming and sexual exploitation.

There is a great imbalance of power between staff and students; the opportunity for people in authority to abuse that power is considerable. As well as making a student feel special, staff can offer students all sorts of tangible benefits including assistance with projects, improved grades and helpful references. Universities have a responsibility to ensure that teaching staff do not abuse their power. Equally important, universities have a duty to ensure that students can always trust the motives of the members of staff who teach them.

Supporters of the status quo argue that it is not appropriate for universities to intrude into the private lives of students and staff. This argument ignores the fact that, in real life, a sexual liaison between a member of staff and a student can never be an entirely private matter. Attempts are usually made to keep the affair secret but this is rarely successful. In time, colleagues and friendship groups begin to suspect what is going on and the nature and legitimacy of the relationship will become a matter of gossip and speculation, particularly on social media. Courses are disrupted as people take sides. Some students will resent the unfair privileges which are assumed to be enjoyed by their colleague and others will blame the member of staff for unprofessional conduct. The vast majority will wish that the relationship had never happened.

Almost all universities which permit sex between staff and students require a member of staff in a sexual relationship with a student to report the liaison to their manager. Disclosure will cause embarrassment and some practical difficulties for the member of staff concerned, so we were not surprised to hear that disclosure rarely takes place until the relationship becomes public knowledge. In fact, delay and avoidance are easy options because the requirement to report is rarely enforced with much vigour. At best, university policies state only that the report should be made 'promptly', whatever that means, and no one who spoke to us could recall disciplinary action being taken against a member of staff who had failed to report.

Once the relationship becomes known to senior management, the university rarely focuses on the welfare of the student. Instead, priority is given to avoiding the conflict of interest which clearly exists when a member of staff is having sex with a student whom they are teaching and assessing. The normal remedy is to transfer the professional responsibilities to another academic. If that is not feasible, the student might be moved to another building, another location or even to another course. Whichever action is chosen, the student's studies will be disrupted and her/his university career is likely to be damaged.

The next crisis occurs when the relationship ends. The break-up is usually accompanied by upset and recrimination. Once again, colleagues and friends will be tempted to take sides and there will be another period of disharmony and distraction. We found that the member of staff will typically get some measure of support from colleagues. Unfortunately the student will often be left without the help and advice which they clearly need, usually regretting the whole experience and having to face an unpleasant backlash, particularly on social media.

When a prohibition of sex between teaching staff and their students is suggested, it is usually pointed out that such relationships are 'sometimes (sic) genuine' and can lead on to stable long-term partnerships and even marriage. No doubt this is true and it is regretted that, for very good reasons, such romances will have to be put on hold until the student's course is completed. However, it should be stressed that almost all the liaisons we have heard about are of a very different kind. The typical story is of a male academic, often married or with a partner, who embarks on an affair which lasts for a few months and frequently ends at the time of the long summer vacation. We were told several stories of men who favour relationships with students in their last year so that graduation provides a convenient break point.

Some of these men are the sort of serial predators whom we described in Chapter 2. Their names are known to the university community (and to us) but they always claim that the sex is consensual and nothing seems to be done to make them stop. A ban on all sexual relationships between teaching staff and their students would give the university an opportunity to put an end to their sexual exploits. We hope that this opportunity will be taken.

Flagship Policy

Against this background, the objections to a prohibition seem rather inconsequential. Universities have very good reasons to insist that, to enhance trust and professionalism, academics should not sleep with their students. Universities are certainly justified in intruding into what some people describe as private matters when the consequences are so serious and damaging. As for the possibility of driving such relationships underground, in reality that is where they already lurk, half-concealed and unregulated, until the tawdry secret is uncovered and an attempt has to be made to deal with the unpleasant consequences.

Contrary to what some managers suggest, drafting fair and workable conditions for a ban is not particularly difficult. An exemption should, of course, be made for relationships which exist before either partner comes to the university. The distinction between staff and student can be based on whether or not an employment contract exists. If students are employed casually on paid work without a contract, this would be a good moment for HR to bring the university into line with good practice.

There may be resistance from some quarters but the case for prohibition is overwhelming and it should become a flagship policy for all higher education. If any university remains unconvinced, the Vice Chancellor should consider the questions which will form in the minds of Ministers, politicians, parents and the general public once it becomes generally known that universities permit their teaching staff to have sex with their students:

- Is a university's permissive attitude to sex between teaching staff and their students consistent with its duty of care to its students?
- Can a sexual relationship between a teacher and a student ever be genuinely consensual or is there always some element of abuse of power?
- Why should a university tolerate behaviour which disrupts work and study and can damage its reputation?
- How can a university tolerate such behaviour by a member of staff when it insists throughout its policies and procedures that the relationship between teaching staff and their students must be based on trust and professionalism?
- How can a university justify moving a student to another course or to another location to avoid a conflict of interest when it is the member of staff who should bear most of the responsibility for causing the problem?

We recommend that universities approach the trade unions to propose that a new contractual condition is introduced banning members of staff from having sex with students for whom they have a professional responsibility. The proposal should, of course, also be discussed with the NUS and with Student Unions. Once the change is agreed, the new rule should be drawn to the attention of all teaching staff and a clear explanation of the new rule should be included in the introductory material sent to all students at the outset of their university career.

Priorities

In this chapter we have suggested five key elements in a programme to reduce sexual harassment and abuse.

1. Commission a survey to establish the extent and nature of sexual harassment and abuse.
2. Give decision-makers direct experience of the misery and distress of victims by arranging for Vice Chancellors to meet and hear reports of their abuse from the lips of victim/survivors.
3. Introduce a separate procedure for the report, investigation and decision on matters of sexual misconduct in accessible and sympathetic language in a single document without the need to cross refer to other regulations and ordinances.
4. Adopt a programme in each university led by the Vice Chancellor and Governing body to transform the sexual culture of their university.
5. Demonstrate the university's professionalism and its duty of care to students by banning sexual relationships between teaching staff and their students.

These five proposals represent a priority list of actions. They are intended to kick-start the substantial reform programme that is needed. If the measures are introduced with commitment, it will soon become apparent that other changes should be made. For instance, every university will need to employ a complement of specialist staff, much more training will be required, high-quality advice should be available on campus at all times, every complainant should have an allocated advisor to provide support throughout the procedure... and much more.[5]

This priority list might also be regarded as a test of good intentions. Universities which press ahead with the reform programme should be assisted and applauded. However, universities which fail to introduce the necessary measures will be giving a clear message to government, parents and to the wider public that they are not sufficiently committed to making their institutions safe places for study and work.

In our next chapter we consider how universities can be encouraged to adopt the necessary reforms. We also consider what action might be taken if they fail to do so.

Appendix

A comprehensive programme to reduce sexual abuse

1. Commission a survey to establish the extent and nature of sexual harassment and abuse.
2. Give decision-makers direct experience of the misery and distress of victims by arranging for Vice Chancellors and senior managers to meet and hear reports of their abuse from the lips of victims.
3. Establish a university-wide approach to sexual abuse which applies to all members of the university community, including students, staff, contractors and visitors.
4. State publicly, clearly and loudly that sexual misconduct is not tolerated in the university.
5. Gain the support and involvement of the trade unions and Student Union in promoting this policy of zero tolerance.
6. Publicise the policy of zero tolerance throughout the university and on social media.
7. Employ a complement of specialist staff to advise on policy, support other advisors and handle difficult cases.
8. Ensure that staff who receive complaints and those who advise and support complainants are well trained.
9. Make high-quality advice available on campus to complainants at all times.
10. Support the policy by arranging training and awareness courses supported by experts from outside the university, like the local Rape Crisis centre, on harassment and consent.

11. Base actions and support on acceptance that the complainant is telling the truth.
12. Make sure that the reporting of sexual abuse is as easy as possible and that advice and sympathetic support are always readily available by establishing a high-profile centre on campus with well-trained staff who can be contacted by 'phone, email, social media or in person'.
13. Allow anonymous reporting to achieve more accurate numbers, greater credibility and knowledge of persistent offenders.
14. Make sure there are no time restrictions on how quickly after the incident a complainant needs to report.
15. Once a report is made, allocate a trained adviser to the complainant and ensure that the adviser is available to support her/him throughout the complaints process.
16. Introduce a separate procedure for the report, investigation and decision on matters of sexual misconduct in accessible and sympathetic language in a single document without the need to cross-refer to other regulations and ordinances.
17. Rewrite the university's regulations and procedures to ensure consistency, to reduce complexity and to avoid any ambiguity about how allegations of sexual misconduct are dealt with.
18. Explain the penalties that perpetrators will suffer.
19. Guarantee the complainant the right to be accompanied to all meetings by her/his adviser and by a friend or representative from the Student Union or her/his trade union.
20. If an alleged perpetrator has substantial advocacy, consider appointing an advocate to represent the complainant.
21. Deal with complaints promptly so that the sexual misconduct procedure reaches a conclusion within one calendar month.
22. Make progress reports to the complainant and inform her/him of the outcome of the complaint at the same time as the alleged perpetrator is told.

23. Demonstrate the university's professionalism and its duty of care to students by banning sexual relationships between staff and students.
24. Each Vice Chancellor and Governing body should adopt a programme to transform the sexual culture of their university.
25. Create a high-level committee with the task of implementing, monitoring and improving the sexual misconduct policy. The Student Union and the trade unions should be represented on the committee.

9

Regulation and Pressure

At the core of the debate about sexual harassment and abuse in higher education is a disagreement about whether the problem should be regarded as a routine matter for universities to manage as well as they can or whether it should be viewed as so serious that outside intervention must be contemplated.

The evidence we have gathered from our interviews and from media reports demonstrates that the problem is very serious. Well-informed observers from outside the university community have reached a similar conclusion. Vera Baird, the Victims Commissioner, points out that the incidence of sexual abuse in universities gives particular cause for concern because it is higher than in the general population.[1]

Using testimony from interviewees, evidence from media reports and from our examination of university processes, we have shown that universities are not coping very well. This judgement is also gaining support. Since about 2015, journalists have begun to look beyond the details of each particular scandal and are now making increasingly severe criticisms of the performance of the higher education sector as a whole. The BBC radio programme, *File on 4*, for instance, found

> serious flaws in the way many universities mismanage (sic) reports of sexual assaults and harassment and how

some students believe they're re-victimised and bullied into keeping their complaints quiet.[2]

External observers have become more sceptical when individual universities or Universities UK (UUK) state that worthwhile improvements are being made. As we noted earlier, when Sarah Green, from the *End Violence Against Women Coalition*, was asked to assess the value of proposals made by UUK to improve the way universities handle complaints of assault, she quickly identified the weaknesses.

> UUK do not propose any mechanism for enforcement, monitoring is left to individual institutions and there are no recommendations to government for a change in the law should universities not comply with the recommendations.[3]

Intervention

These comments by Sarah Green take us to the heart of the matter. Each university is able to make its own independent decision about the importance it attaches to sexual harassment and abuse. It designs its own policies, decides its own procedures and determines the nature of enforcement. This explains the wide differences which exist between the performance of individual universities. Some are working hard to make major improvements, others are doing rather less and a number seem be giving the issue little attention.

A successful policy to reduce sexual harassment and abuse across the sector requires coordination and collective action. Unfortunately there is no structure in place to ensure that universities act in concert or even adopt the same policies. UUK is the main organisation which represents universities in general. It produces valuable reports but it has no power to require reluctant members to adopt any of its recommendations. UUK has to proceed by consensus but, because of the differences in attitudes which we found in our examination of university policies and procedures, building a common policy to combat sexual harassment and abuse is difficult. Like most membership organisations UUK tends to move at the pace of the slowest vessel in the convoy. On the basis of past performance, the pace is likely to be stately rather than urgent.

The poor record of so many universities in dealing with sexual harassment and abuse has prompted calls for intervention by Government. We heard many such suggestions from the people we interviewed. And with growing media interest, the pressure for Government to take some degree of control is likely to increase.

Unfortunately, while it is easy to demand Government intervention, it is much more difficult to propose a method of intervention which is likely to prove effective. National Government probably knows less about how to deal with sexual harassment and abuse in higher education than even the most poorly performing university. In the absence of detailed knowledge and understanding, Government action is likely to be clumsy and ill-directed. In any event, as we argued in Chapter 8, a major problem in many universities is the lack of motivation. Government intervention might produce a minimum level of compliance but it is unlikely to convince reluctant managers that they should become enthusiastic about solving a problem which they have neglected for so long. And if Government intervention leads to cynicism about ministerial motives and to accusations that politicians are interfering in university internal affairs, the resulting row could make matters worse.

For all these reasons we are not inclined to support a policy of general intervention by Government. However, we make one exception.

An Authoritative Survey

Throughout this book we have argued that the most urgent requirement in the battle to reduce sexual harassment and abuse is for universities to commission an authoritative survey which establishes the true extent and nature of the problem. To be effective, future policy decisions must be based on reliable evidence rather than on guesswork and speculation.

The Government should also appreciate that there is a strong public interest case for commissioning a survey which would give students and staff reliable information about the risks they face and give members of the public a much-needed insight into the higher education system which they help to fund.

In Chapter 8 we demonstrated that an authoritative survey is affordable. What seems to be lacking is any determination in higher education to make it happen. If universities do not move quickly, there is a strong case for the Government to intervene and require action from the sector.

The Minister concerned can be confident that if s/he needs to make this limited but crucial intervention, s/he is likely to receive strong backing from the public, from other politicians and from the media.

The Regulators

Once it is accepted that Government should only intervene selectively, the key question is what alternative pressure can be applied to ensure that universities greatly improve their performance in reducing sexual harassment and abuse.

It has been suggested to us that the most appropriate organisations to stimulate the introduction of the necessary reforms and to encourage concerted action across the university sector are the

Office for Students (OfS), the regulator of higher education in England and its equivalent in the Welsh Government.

The OfS is charged with a responsibility to

> 'protect the interests of students, short, medium and long term.'

OfS has intimate knowledge of how universities operate and has significant authority. In principle it seems to be the ideal organisation to take on the task of encouraging and requiring universities to clear up what has become a deplorable mess.

Although it has a responsibility for the well-being of students, until recently OfS has concentrated on other matters. OfS is a relatively new organisation[4], and it is perhaps understandable that its initial focus has been on major existential issues like university structures and financial viability. However, when we examined its Regulatory Framework, OfS's major policy document, we expected to find details of the standards which OfS intended to set for the welfare of university students. We found none. Although the OfS's Regulatory Framework runs to 164 pages, the word 'welfare' never appears.

We looked for some indication that OfS is urging universities to eradicate sexual misconduct. Again we were disappointed. The words 'sex', 'sexual' and 'harassment' are never used. The word 'abuse' occurs once but only in the context of an abuse of funds. These omissions seem very odd in the light of OfS's declared wish that every student should

> 'have a fulfilling experience of higher education that enriches their lives and careers.'[5]

It is obvious from the testimony we received from very many victim/survivors that this noble objective can only be achieved if students are properly protected from sexual harassment and abuse.

We are not experts on the regulatory process, so we took further advice. In fact the explanation for these apparently surprising omissions from OfS's Regulatory Framework is very simple. Although OfS has a responsibility to encourage good welfare provisions, it does not have the legal authority to require universities to apply particular welfare standards. OfS can encourage universities to adopt good practice but it cannot make student welfare part of its regulatory framework.

This is very disappointing and, in our view, there should be an early change in the OfS's remit. OfS cannot be regarded as an effective guardian of student welfare unless it is given the legal powers to enforce the necessary standards.

Fortunately there are strong indications that OfS itself recognises that the present situation is unsatisfactory. Nicola Dandridge, Chief Executive of OfS, sets out the Office's concerns in these terms:

> 'There are a great number of things a new student might think about when arriving at a university or college. Concerns about harassment, hate crime or sexual misconduct should not be one of them. But the fact is these issues are far too common. Worse still, too many students say they are not getting the support they need if they suffer this unacceptable behaviour.'[6]

She went on to add that:

> 'Our immediate focus is to make sure our expectations as the regulator are clear about what it is universities and colleges should be doing to prevent harassment, hate crime and sexual misconduct, and to deal with reports appropriately and effectively.'[7]

At the beginning of 2020, OfS went further and issued a statement critical of the way universities handle complaints of sexual misconduct. It declared that students who have been sexually assaulted or harassed are often let down by 'inadequate' support and 'ineffective' reporting arrangements. OfS called on universities to have robust procedures to address complaints of sexual abuse and to ensure that students know how to report their concerns.

The statement included a warning. to universities that they could face sanctions, including fines and deregulation, if they fail to respond to reports of sexual misconduct.[8]

This is good news. As we explained in chapter 1, when Nicola Dandridge was Chief Executive of UUK, she chaired the Taskforce which produced Changing the Culture,[9] the first report which acknowledged that universities need to improve their performance in reducing sexual misconduct. Her background knowledge and experience puts her in a good position to lead the initiative by OfS to require higher standards from universities.

However, some universities are reluctant to reform and if the clear warning to universities issued by OfS does not produce the necessary improvements, we trust that OfS will recommend a change in its legal powers so that it can require universities to achieve specific standards as part of its regulatory regime.

There is no equivalent to OfS in Wales. Funding is regulated by the Higher Education Funding Council for Wales but the responsibility for student welfare rests with the Welsh Government. We hope that the Minister for Education in Wales will ensure that her/his officials maintain close contact with OfS and that the standards required of Welsh universities in handling complaints and reducing sexual misconduct are at least as high as those in England.

Public Agencies

The regulators in England and Wales will need to work with vigour and determination, but we recognise that, working alone, their task will be formidable. Satisfactory outcomes are more likely to be achieved if other organisations in the public and private sectors, and in civil society, actively support the regulators in pressing universities to do better.

We have referred to the impressive work of Public Health England in Chapter 7 and it might stand as a model for other agencies. In 2016 it published '*A review of evidence for bystander intervention to prevent sexual and domestic violence in universities*'.[10]

The Review begins by explaining Public Health England's interest.

> 'Violence against women is a critical concern for public health and human rights. There is a growing body of evidence from UK universities adding to the international evidence base documenting that universities are significant sites for violence against women. Universities in the UK are increasingly motivated to seek effective long-term solutions.'

Relying heavily on US research and experience, the review concluded that bystander intervention has the potential to change behaviour and, properly introduced, might contribute to a welcome change in culture. As we explained in Chapter 7, the aim of bystander intervention is to create a corps of volunteers who are trained to recognise situations where people are at risk and to take action to reduce that risk.

Dr Rachel Fenton of The University of Exeter was deeply involved in producing the Review and she has subsequently led the Intervention Initiative. According to Dr Fenton, it has been used in about 50 universities throughout the country to train students.

The Intervention Initiative has been recommended by UUK and their most recent report[11] describes bystander training as,

> 'the most common initiative being rolled out across the sector.'

This represents a significant success, and we looked for other public agencies which might add their support and prompt universities to implement other useful initiatives.

In particular we hope that the Equality and Human Rights Commission (EHRC) will launch an enquiry into sexual abuse in universities. The Commission is very familiar with the issue of sexual abuse, having produced a detailed report on Sexual Harassment at Work. It is also familiar with the difficulties which universities experience in dealing with harassment. In October 2019 it published the results of its enquiry into Racial Harassment in Higher Education. The findings were very disturbing and captured a good deal of publicity.

> 'Around a quarter of students from an ethnic minority background (24%), and 9% of white students, said they had experienced racial harassment since starting their course. This equates to 13% of all students. 20% of students had been physically attacked. 56% of students who had been racially harassed had experienced racist name-calling, insults and jokes.'[12]

UUK did not dispute the findings. Professor Julia Buckingham, the President of UUK, issued a statement saying,

> 'All higher education providers must study this report's findings and recommendations and take urgent action.
>
> There is no place for racial harassment on a university campus, or anywhere else – and I find it sad and shocking how many people are still subject to it.'[13]

Although we know, from our discussion with her, that Julia Buckingham would not support any reduction in the priority which universities give to their sexual harassment and abuse work, we are concerned that – faced with this very critical report from EHRC – some universities might be tempted to divert resources away from action to reduce sexual harassment and abuse and concentrate on initiatives to combat racism. This would be extremely damaging and completely inappropriate.

We wrote to EHRC asking if it has plans to conduct a similar enquiry into sexual abuse in universities. When the Commission told us that it had no such plans, we wrote again urging an enquiry. We intend to send our research to EHRC and trust that our findings will help to persuade the Commission to undertake an enquiry into sexual harassment and abuse in universities in the near future.

Research Organisations

The funding which comes from research institutes is very important to universities, and departmental managers are sensitive to the requirements of the major funders. So we are very encouraged to learn of the decision by the Wellcome Foundation to take a much closer interest in the culture of the universities it supports.

In 2018 the Wellcome Foundation published a policy document[14] setting out how it expected universities and other grant-receiving institutes to handle issues of bullying and harassment. Wellcome makes a number of recommendations about the need to have complaints and disciplinary procedures in place, which universities will have little difficulty in meeting. However, a number of the requirements go further. Wellcome requires that

'When an organisation submits a grant application to us, they must confirm that the lead applicant (and sponsor and supervisor if relevant), has not had an allegation of bullying or harassment upheld against them for which there is either a current formal disciplinary warning or an active sanction. If they have, we may reject the application.'[15]

In addition,

'if the applicant is new to the organisation, we expect the organisation to check with the previous employer.'[16]

The Wellcome Foundation also requires grant-receiving organisations to tell them when a bullying and harassment investigation has been launched. Wellcome says it expects organisations to complete all investigations which they start, even if the subject of the investigation leaves the university.

The policy also includes a reference to non-disclosure agreements (NDAs) which demonstrates that the Wellcome Foundation will not accept the use of NDAs to deny it relevant information.

'We now discourage (NDAs) that stop organisations sharing the findings of investigations with us.'[17]

Wellcome clearly wants to know much more of what is going on, and this is helpful in encouraging universities to tighten up their procedures. Of course, it is theoretically possible to get round these restrictions. It has even been suggested that the new strictures might make universities less likely to take disciplinary action against high-profile researchers for fear of disqualifying them from making funding applications. We do not take that cynical view. Apart from the dishonesty of such an approach, a university which acts outside the spirit of the rules will face a heavy penalty, both in loss of research funding and in damage to its reputation, once the

Wellcome Foundation or other funders find out. Wellcome intends to review and refine its guidelines. This process will no doubt close loopholes and might, by stages, increase the extent of disclosure.

This initiative by a major research organisation is very helpful in demonstrating to senior managers that a university culture which allows harassment and abuse not only damages the research environment but can also have serious financial consequences. Wellcome seems to have started a useful trend. Cancer Research and the British Heart Foundation have also decided to ensure that research which they are funding takes place in university departments which maintain reasonable standards of behaviour. We trust that other organisations which fund university research of all kinds will follow the lead set by these three prestigious institutions.

Internal Pressure

Events in the entertainment industries and elsewhere have shown that publicity about the extent of abuse puts pressure on decision-makers to give greater attention to sexual misconduct and to work much harder to reduce it. Similar pressure is building up in higher education. As we noted in Chapter 4, a new high-profile story about sexual harassment and abuse in universities now seems to appear in the media at least once a month.

What helped to turn media stories about the film industry from prurient voyeurism into a force for public good were the campaigns. #MeToo and others amplified the publicity and made particular demands for changes in attitudes and behaviour. A similar national campaign is needed in universities.

Local campaigns have achieved success in Leicester and Bristol and in a number of other universities. In Leicester #MeTooOnCampus has won changes in procedures and security, including the recruitment of more counsellors and the introduction of better procedures to ban miscreants, following bad behaviour at social events. At the University of Bristol, women students have used Snapchat to share their stories of sexual assault and harassment in a bid to raise awareness. A video has been produced to demonstrate the extent of the problem.

We have also been told of a number of local campaigns by Student Unions, which have brought tangible improvements. Two conferences have been held in London and Manchester which were clearly helpful to those who attended.

However, these local activities and events have not, so far, coalesced into a national campaign. Individual universities have been encouraged to make changes but few have felt under the sort of pressure which national campaigns have mobilised in other sectors. There is little doubt that the absence of a robust national campaign in universities is an important reason why the pace of reform has been slow and progress has been so patchy.

Of course, the difficulties which students face in forming and sustaining a country-wide campaign are considerable. Most students attend university for only three years. Every year, experienced and confident campaigners graduate and leave. Networks weaken as key personnel move on. So student campaign groups have to be in a constant state of renewal. Social media can spread information, generate activity and publicise events but successful campaigns rely for much of their strength on the mutual trust which is most effectively built by working together over time. We have met exceptional individuals who formed the backbone of student activity while in higher education but their time there is short and they are difficult to replace.

Alongside student campaigns are activities run by academics. GenPol is a think tank and social enterprise. It acts as an advocate for gender equality and promotes the understanding of gender and seeks gender-sensitive solutions to cultural problems. GenPol has done valuable work in advocating comprehensive sex and relationship education as a crucial means of counteracting gender-based violence. Its aims are very specific. It promotes policies which decision-makers can use to change culture and behaviour but it does not confront senior managers in universities (and schools) directly. Quite deliberately it is a resource rather than a campaign in the normal sense and it relies on practitioners to implement its recommendations. This sometimes leads to the sort of frustration which has frequently been expressed by experts who have spoken to us. With careful understatement, GenPol comments that:

> '... successfully delivering educational tools on the themes of gender, informed consent and every form of violence, often eludes policy-makers.'[18]

The 1752 Group

The 1752 Group is very different. In December 2015, a number of academics organised the first British university conference which discussed the sexual harassment and abuse of students by members of staff. It was held at Goldsmiths, London University, and led to the formation of a national organisation to address that issue. The unusual name was adopted by the Group as a reference to the sum of £1752 which was allocated to fund that first conference.

The 1752 Group is now led by four academics, supported by an Advisory Board of academics together with a representative of the NUS, a partner from solicitors McAllister Olivarius, the Director of End Violence Against Women and two other external specialists.

From its inception, 1752 has concentrated on the sexual harassment and abuse of students by staff. It does not focus on the harassment and abuse of students by other students. It explains this approach by pointing out that sexual abuse of students by members of university staff is,

> 'under-reported and under-researched.'[19]

This sharp focus has brought some significant benefits. By publishing useful articles and reports, 1752 has helped to illuminate a murky area of university life. Perhaps its two most important pieces of work are the April 2018 joint report with NUS, *'Power in the Academy: staff sexual misconduct in UK higher education'* and the report with solicitors, McAllister Olivarius, which made recommendations for disciplinary processes arising from complaints by students of sexual abuse by members of university staff.[20]

This is an impressive record of achievement. In the last few years there has been the significant change of public attitudes to sexual abuse which we described in Chapter 4. With the media becoming much more interested in what is going on in universities, there is a real opportunity for progress. Perhaps the 1752 Group might consider that this would be the right moment to extend the scope of their lobbying and research to include all sexual harassment and abuse in universities. 1752 could use its knowledge and experience to provide a campaigning hub to focus the work which is taking place locally but which has so far lacked a national profile.

Pressure from the Unions

The final element of pressure should come from the unions – both the trade unions and the Student Unions. Its mobilising effect could be conclusive in creating a safer place to work and study.

Four trade unions represent university employees. The University and College Union (UCU) represents academic and academic-related staff. GMB, Unison and Unite the Union represent support staff.

All four unions have strong policies on sexual harassment and abuse at work. They are all part of the #ThisIsNotWorking alliance, a coalition led by the TUC which includes over 30 trade unions and women's rights organisations. The alliance is,

> 'calling for a new, easily enforceable legal duty that would require employers to take all reasonable steps to protect workers from sexual harassment and victimisation.'[21]

The four trade unions each give detailed advice to their members about how to deal with harassment and abuse, including information on whom to contact for support, how to report abuse, how to pursue a complaint and how to secure union representation. The UCU takes the issue of sexual abuse particularly seriously. It has a strongly worded policy issued by its governing body, issues guidance for branches and members, has drafted a model agreement and has set up a dedicated Sexual Harassment Support Helpline.

The NUS represents students in Student Unions across the country. It has a strong tradition of campaigning against sexual harassment and abuse in universities. It has published a series of reports on sexual abuse including *Hidden Marks* in 2010, *That's What She Said* in 2014 (with Alison Phipps), *Power in the Academy* in 2018 (with the 1752 Group) and *Sexual Violence in Further Education* in 2019. These reports provide some of the best information which is currently available about sexual misconduct and its effects in higher and further education. NUS has used the findings from the reports to campaign for more committed action by universities, more trained and specialist support staff, better protection for victim/survivors and for an end to so-called 'lad culture'.

This is very valuable work and it encourages a strong feeling that sustained pressure can be applied. Unfortunately the trade unions and the NUS face the familiar difficulty which has hampered all attempts to reduce sexual harassment and abuse by concerted action. Every university seems determined to maintain their right to independent action. So instead of taking a collective approach and expecting a collective response from universities, trade unions and the NUS find themselves having to persuade each university separately to take the necessary action. The process is time consuming, the outcome is bound to be messy and progress on each issue tends to be patchy and slow.

Coalition

In these circumstances the best tactic is to avoid making a host of proposals, narrow the scope of debate by selecting a limited number of key issues and aim to build a coalition of support around that limited programme.

In the previous chapter we proposed five key campaigning issues:

1. An authoritative survey should be commissioned to establish the extent and nature of sexual harassment and abuse

2. Meetings should be organised so that Vice Chancellors hear directly from victim/survivors

3. A separate procedure should be introduced to deal with the particular issue of sexual harassment and abuse, recognising the specific needs of complainants

4. A programme should be initiated in each university and led by the Vice Chancellor to transform the sexual culture of the institution

5. Sexual relationships between teaching staff and their students should prohibited in all universities.

We chose these five issues not only because they would make campuses much safer for students and staff but also because they would generate momentum for further reforms. We hope that some or all of these proposals might be adopted as the programme advocated by a coalition of unions and other reforming groups.

The coalition of support should be as wide as possible. We believe that GenPol, 1752 and many local campaign groups could be persuaded of the benefits of the programme. Some of the embryonic parent groups should be approached. The TUC would almost certainly offer support and some politicians might be prepared to give their backing. These endorsements from outside the higher education sector would become particularly valuable if the universities give an unhelpful response and the campaign has to move into the political arena.

A starting point might be to ask the EHRC to conduct a full enquiry into sexual harassment and abuse in universities, as we suggested earlier in this chapter. A useful next step would be to lay the evidence from this book and other sources before the Education Select Committee of the House of Commons and to request the Committee to schedule a study of sexual harassment and abuse in universities as part of its work in the next session of Parliament. These initiatives could run alongside the discussions with UUK. The aim should be to convince universities that the pressure for reform will continue to build until effective action is taken.

Leadership

Of course, a better outcome would be for universities to avoid all the criticism and pressure by recognising their responsibilities and, instead of reacting to regulation and pressure, take a leadership role themselves. In our next and final chapter we argue that universities should review their current work, accept the need for radical change and make a fresh start.

10

Starting Afresh

In this book we have told the story of a tragedy.

Every person we interviewed, Vice Chancellors, academics, students and the rest, want universities to be places of safety, entirely free from sexual harassment and abuse. Every set of procedures we examined carried a commitment to create a community based on the values of humanity, dignity and respect. Every manager we met described the work which was being done to combat sexual abuse.

And yet, by a very conservative estimate, about 50,000 students and an unknown number of staff suffer sexual harassment and abuse at university every year. Victim/survivors told us of their distress: first the horrible ordeal and then the woeful after-effects which can last for weeks, months and sometimes forever. Confidence is shattered, suspicion replaces trust, ambition is blunted and careers are damaged.

The failures which we have identified in university policies and practice are layered one upon another: failures of will, failures of judgement and failures of process.

Universities know that they must do better. They have a responsibility to take sexual misconduct far more seriously, to base their policies on deeper knowledge and implement them with greater care.

If they are to succeed, universities need:

- good quality information about the extent and nature of sexual harassment and abuse;
- trained specialists to frame the policy and guide its implementation;
- effective and well-motivated managers.

At present, much of this does not exist. Every university lacks reliable data, most do not employ trained specialists and far too many make do with undertrained and inexperienced managers.

In fact, there are so many gaps to fill and so many changes to make that it would be best to start afresh with a newly designed programme of protection and support.

Universities have a clear duty of care to their students and staff. Many people in the university community would also acknowledge that they have a role which is deeper and wider. The Universities and College Union (UCU), the union that represents teachers and researchers in universities, puts it like this:

> 'The transformative power of education gives us a particular responsibility to confront and challenge violence and harassment within our union and across our colleges and universities.'[1]

We argued in Chapter 7 that the power of education to transform lives must reach well beyond our campuses. The revelations of the last few years have shown just how far the culture of Britain is polluted by false notions of sexual entitlement and by a currency of disrespect. Radical change is desperately needed, not just in universities but throughout our society.

In theory at least, universities are in the best position to lead us out of this cultural impasse. They have the task and privilege of educating many of the people who, in time, will hold prominent positions in this country and will set the standards for acceptable behaviour.

If those students experience in university a community where not just sexual relationships but all social intercourse in based on consent and respect, and where concern for the dignity of others is a guiding principle in all human activity, there is a good chance that Britain will become a happier and more civilised country.

So a great deal rests on the actions which universities now take. At present they are on the defensive, under-performing, apologising for the latest scandal and hoping for the best. However, some universities are showing greater ambition and that is a better way forward for the whole sector. Universities should aim to be exemplars, leading the way on these cultural issues – not just trying to reduce sexual harassment and abuse but searching for the reasons why misconduct is so prevalent and exploring how the attitudes that sustain it can be changed.

That is why we recommend a fresh start. Universities face a great challenge but, although at the moment it seems well-disguised, there is also a considerable opportunity. By getting out of its own mess, higher education can show how our culture might be changed for the better. Universities should look beyond damage limitation and consider how their struggles on campus might help the wider community to a better life.

NOTES

Chapter 1: A Scandal Concealed

1. *Guardian*, 25 June 2019 by Richard J Evans.

2. Introduction to *Lucky Jim*, Kingsley Amis, Penguin, 2000 edition.

3. *Hidden Marks: A study of women students' experiences of harassment, stalking and sexual assault*, NUS, 2010.

4. *Telegraph*, 29 July 2015.

5. *Telegraph*, 14 January 2015.

6. Professor Kevin Fenton, Director of Health and Wellbeing at Public Health England, January 2015.

7. *Telegraph*, 14 January 2015.

8. Particularly in the *Independent*.

9. *Guardian*, 7 October 2016.

10. Research by BROOK and their arm DigIn Published: 25 February 2019.

11. *SUN*, 30 January 2017.

12. *Hidden Marks*, NUS, 2010.

13. NUS/1752 report.

14. 14 March 2018, *The gryphon* Web Editor.

15. *Hidden Marks*, NUS, 2010.

16. *Power in the Academy, Staff sexual misconduct in higher education*, NUS and 1752 Group, 2018.

17. *Changing the Culture: Report of the universities UK taskforce examining violence against women, harassment and hate crime affecting university students*, UUK, 2016.

18. *ACAS guidance on sexual harassment in the Workplace*, 2017.

19. *Tackling gender-based violence, harassment and hate crime: Two years on*, Universities UK, 2019.

20. Commissioner Kate Jenkins at launch of Australian human rights commission report into sexual abuse in universities, 1 August 2017.

21. *Changing the culture: Report of the universities UK Taskforce examining violence against women, harassment and hate crime affecting university students*, Universities UK, 2016.

22. *Times HES*, 4 August 2017.

23. This happens quite often. For instance, a report on sexual abuse at Lloyd's of London was said to have left the chief executive, 'devastated' by the extent of the problem. *Guardian*, 19 September 2019.

24. Reports in *The Telegraph, Times, Guardian* and *Financial Times* and on BBC News throughout Spring and Summer of 2018.

25. *Physics Today* 71, 2018.

26. BBC News, 17 April 2019.

27. Speech at LSE, May 2019.

Chapter 2: Stories of Distress

1. BBC Radio 4, 3 October 2019.

2. *Changing the Culture: Report of the universities UK taskforce examining violence against women, harassment and hate crime affecting university students*, UUK, 2016.

3. *Changing the Culture*, UUK, 2016.

4. *Changing the Culture*, UUK, 2016.

5. *That's What She Said*, NUS, 2013.

6. *Hidden Marks: A study of women students' experiences of harassment, stalking and sexual assault*, NUS, 2010.

7. *Changing the Culture*, UUK, 2016.

8. *Changing the Culture*, UUK, 2016.

9. BBC News, 31 January 2019, quoting the Warwick University student newspaper, *The Boar*.

10. *Neoliberalisation and 'Lad cultures'* in Higher Education, Alison Phipps and Isobel Young, Sociology, 2015.

11. *Why are so many well intentioned people still quiet on the ethics of porn? Guardian*, 15 August 2019.

12. *Slow Motion: Changing masculinities, changing men.* Lynn Segal, Virago, 1990.

13. *Posh Boys: How the English Public Schools Run Britain*, Robert Verkaik, Oneworld, 2018.

14. *Posh Boys: How the English Public Schools Run Britain*, Robert Verkaik, Oneworld, 2018.

15. *Posh Boys: How the English Public Schools Run Britain*, Robert Verkaik, Oneworld, 2018.

16. *The Beer Talking: four lads, a carry out and the reproduction of masculinities.* Brendan Gough and Gareth, 1 August 1998.

17. *The Beer Talking: four lads, a carry out and the reproduction of masculinities.* Brendan Gough and Gareth, 1 August 1998.

18. *Sexism at the Centre: Locating the problem of sexual harassment.* Leila Whitely and Tiffany Page, New Formations, 2015.

19. *A very private affair*, Pam Carter and Tony Jeffs, Education New Books, 1995.

20. *A very private affair*, Pam Carter and Tony Jeffs, Education New Books, 1995.

21. *Hidden Marks*, NUS, 2010.

22. *Sexism at the Centre*, New Formations, 2015.

23. Quoted from authors' interview with Elish Angiolini.

24. *A Woman's Work*, Harriet Harman, Allen Lane, 2017.

25. 21 October 2018.

26. *The Stalled Revolution*, Eva Tutchell and John Edmonds, Emerald, 2018.

27. *The Times*, 6 July 2019.

28. *Sexual Assault: What happens after students speak out?* BBC podcast, August 2019.

29. *Hidden Marks*, NUS, 2010.

30. BBC News, 16 September 2019.

31. *Today Programme*, Radio 4, 2 August 2019.

Chapter 3: Doubts and Discontent

1. *Independent*, 20 October 1993.

2. *Final Report of the Taskforce on Student Disciplinary Procedures*, Council of Vice-Chancellors and Principals, 1994.

3. *Final Report of the Taskforce on Student Disciplinary Procedures*, Council of Vice-Chancellors and Principals, 1994.

4. *Final Report of the Taskforce on Student Disciplinary Procedures*, Council of Vice-Chancellors and Principals, 1994.

5. *Final Report of the Taskforce on Student Disciplinary Procedures*, Council of Vice-Chancellors and Principals, 1994.

6. UUK Conference, 8 November 2017.

7. *Guidance for Higher Education Institutions. How to handle alleged student misconduct which may also constitute a criminal offence*, Pinsent Masons and Universities UK, 2016.

8. BBC News, October 2016.

9. *The Guardian*, 5 March 2017.

10. Jennifer J. Freyd, Professor of Psychology, University of Oregon, 11 January 2018.

11. *Huck Magazine*, posted 22 March 2017.

12. *Power in the Academy: Staff Sexual Misconduct in UK Higher Education*, NUS and 1752, 2018.

Chapter 4: Evidence from the Media

1. *Telegraph*, 14 January 2015.

2. Independent, 15 August 2016.

3. *Independent Review into Sussex's Response to Domestic Violence*, Professor Nicole Westmarland, 2017.

4. Independent Review into Sussex"s Response to Domestic Violence, Professor Nicole Westmarland, 2017.

5. Independent Review into Sussex"s Response to Domestic Violence, Professor Nicole Westmarland, 2017.

6. *Independent*, 18 January 2017 and Argus, 17 January amongst others.

7. *Telegraph*, 9 June 2016.

8. *The Times*, 28 July 2018 and Guardian, 22 January 2019.

9. *Sun*, 27 January 2017.

10. *Mirror*, 20 January 2017.

11. The Snapchat report was organised by #RevoltAgainstSexualAssault led by Hannah Price, at that time a final year mathematics student.

12. *Daily Mail*, 18 May 2017.

13. *Guardian*, 5 February 2018.

14. *The Times*, 2 June 2019.

15. *Evening Standard*, 3 July 2018.

16. *BBC News*, 29 May 2019.

17. *The Times*, 6 July 2019.

18. *Guardian*, 11 August 2019.

19. BBC; File on 4, 22 September 2019.

20. BBC, 3 October 2019.

21. *Guardian*, 7 November 2019.

22. Observer, 22 February 2020.

23. Guardian, 18 November 2019.

24. Telegraph, 23 February 2020.

25. Telegraph, 23 February 2020.

26. Church Times, 4 March 2020.

27. Guardian, 19 April 2020.

28. BBC report, 3 October 2019.

Chapter: 5: A Failing Process

1. We also wrote to 10 colleges in Cambridge and Oxford to establish whether colleges are following procedures which are different from the procedures which operate at university level.

2. For instance, the Labour Party's *Sexual Harassment Policy and Procedure*, adopted January 2019.

3. Clause A23 of this university's Student Complaints Procedure.

4. *Hidden Marks*, NUS, 2010.

5. The law prohibits teachers in schools, colleges and universities from having sex with one of their students if the student is under the age of 18 years.

6. We found that the Principal of St Hugh's College, Oxford warns students in her welcome speech against such behaviour. See Chapter 2, page 38.

Chapter 6: Living with the Market

1. *ManMade: Why so few women are in positions of power*, Eva Tutchell and John Edmonds, Gower, 2015.

2. ITN figures for 2017/2018 published in March 2018.

3. The Arts Council of England diversity report, 2017–2018.

4. Universities need to promote more women to professor, *Guardian*, 8 March 2019.

5. Interview for 'The Life Scientific', Radio 4, 25 October 2011.

6. *Quoted in Ninette de Valois's theories of dance*, by Genne, Beth. Article appears in Ninette de Valois; *Adventurous traditionalist*, Cave R. and Worth L., Dance books, 2012.

7. *ManMade*, Eva Tutchell and John Edmonds, Gower, 2015.

8. Higher education staff statistics, UK 2017/2018. HESA, 24 January 2019.

9. Hinds, Damian, Secretary the State for Education, interview with i newspaper, 23 May 2019.

10. *Inside Higher Education*, 14 March 2018.

11. Neoliberalism and 'Lad Cultures' in Higher Education by Alison Phipps and Isobel Young in Sociology, Vol 49, Issue 2, 2015.

12. NUS.

13. *Hidden Marks: A study of women students' experiences of harassment, stalking and sexual assault*, NUS, 2010.

14. www.empowered campus.co.uk.

15. Neoliberalism, op. cit.

16. *Quoted in Mask Off*, JJ Bola, Pluto Press, 2019.

17. *The Telegraph*, 8 October 2014.

18. *BBC News*, October 2014.

19. Re-theorising laddish masculinities in higher education, Alison Phipps, *Gender and Education 29*, 2017.

20. *The Beer Talking: four lads, a carry out and the reproduction of masculinities*, Brendan Gough and Gareth, 1 August 1998.

21. *The Beer Talking*, Brendan Gough and Gareth, 1 August 1998.

22. Queer decisions? Gay male students' university choices in Studies in *Higher Education volume 35* May 2010 and assertion, regulations, consent: gay students, straight flatmates, and the (hetero) sexualisation of university accommodation space, Richard Taulke-Johnson, *Gender in Education Vol. 22*, February 2010.

23. *Pimp State: Sex, money and the future of equality*, Kat Banyard, Faber and Faber, 2016.

24. *Irish Times*, 25 June 2018.

25. *Porn is everywhere*, Children's Commissioner, 30 June 2010.

26. The effects of porn on adolescent boys, Alexandra Katehatis, *Psychology Today*, 28 July, 2011.

27. *Pimp State*, Kat Banyard, Faber and Faber, 2016.

28. *Sexism at the Centre: Locating the problem of sexual harassment*, Leila Whitely and Tiffany Page, New Formations, 2015.

29. *Guardian*, 5 March 2017.

30. *Guardian*, 5 March 2017.

31. *ManMade*, Eva Tutchell and John Edmonds, Gower, 2015.

32. *ManMade*, Eva Tutchell and John Edmonds, Gower, 2015.

33. *Independent*, 11 August 2017.

34. *Bloomberg*, 7 August 2019.

35. *Guardian*, 11 June 2017.

36. *Independent*, 11 August 2017.

37. *Guardian*, 31 July 2019.

Chapter 7: Seeking a Better Culture

1. Website of Women and Gender Advocacy Centre.

2. *Slow motion: changing masculinities, changing men*, Lynn Segal, Virago, 1990.

3. Evidence gained from buying cards congratulating new parents.

4. *Slow motion*, Lynn Segal, 1990.

5. *The Sexuality of Men*, edited by Andy Metcalfe and Martin Humphries, Pluto Press, 1985.

6. *Male sexuality: How men feel about sex and love*, Shere Hite, reprinted by various publishers, 1981.

7. *What is to be done about violence against women*, Elizabeth Wilson, Penguin Books, 1983.

8. *Slow motion: changing masculinities*, Lynn Segal, 1990.

9. *Men and Masculinity*, Pleck and Sawyer, Prentice Hall, 1975.

10. *The Sexuality of men*, edited by Andy Metcalfe and Martin Humphries, Pluto Press, 1985.

11. *Mask Off – masculinity redefined*, JJ Bola, Pluto Press, 2019.

12. *The Telegraph*, 25 September 2019.

13. *Pimp State: Sex, Money and the Future of Equality*. Kat Banyard, Faber and Faber, 2016.

14. Tony Eardley, writing in *The Sexuality of Men*, edited by Andy Metcalfe and Martin Humphries, Pluto Press, 1985.

15. *The Sexuality of Men*, Andy Metcalfe and Martin Humphries, 1985.

16. *ManMade: Why so few women are in positions of power*, Eva Tutchell and John Edmonds, Gower, 2015.

17. All national newspapers, 21 June 2019.

18. *Male pastors read Sexist comments people made to their female colleagues*, Huffpost, 19 June 2019.

19. *Boris Johnson: A tale of blond ambition*, Sonia Purnell, Autumn Press 2012.

20. *Misogyny, feminism and sexual harassment*, Kalpana Srivastava et al., Industrial Psychiatry Journal, Vol 26, Issue 2, 2017.

21. *Hidden Marks: A Study of Women Students' Experiences of Harassment, Stalking and Sexual Assault*, NUS, 2010.

22. *Changing the culture: Report of the Universities UK Taskforce examining violence against women, harassment and hate crime affecting university students*. Universities UK, 2016.

23. *Being a Boy, Julius Lester from Heart of a Man: Men's Stories for Women*, edited by Bill Amatneek, Vineyards Press, 2019.

24. Tony Eardley in *The Sexuality of Men*, op.cit.

25. *Modern Masculinity*, Imam Amrani, Guardian, 14 August 2019.

26. *The Conversation*, 27 March 2019.

27. *Slow motion: changing masculinities*, Lynn Segal, 1990.

28. *Mask off*, JJ Bola, Pluto Press, 2019.

29. *https.trainingcentre.unwomen.org*.

30. Report by American College of Obstetricians, 28 March 2019.

31. Bustle: Planned Parenthood website, 11 August 2016.

32. Let's talk about consent, UCL news, 20 June 2019.

33. 10 July 2018.

34. RSE (Relationship and sex education) is compulsory for all schools from September 2020.

35. The *Money's Good, the Fame's good, the girls are good'*, John Swain, British Journal of Sociology Vol 21 Issue 1 2000.

36. *Bill's New Frock*, Anne Fine, Methuen, 1989.

37. *The Turbulent Term of Tyke Tiler*, Gene Kemp, Faber 1977.

38. *Mindset: The new psychology of success*, Carol Dweck, Ballantine Books 2006.

39. *You and me: the neuroscience of identity*, Susan Greenfield, Notting Hlll Editions, 2011.

40. *Mindset: The new psychology of success*, Carol Dweck, Ballantine Books 2006.

41. *A Theory of Personality: the psychology of personal constructs.*, George Kelly, WW Norton and Company, 1955.

42. *The Language of hypothesis*, George Kelly, New York Wiley, 1964.

Chapter 8: Ending the Abuse

1. The other major organisations which represent universities are MillionPlus and Guild of Higher Education (GuildHE).

2. *File on 4*, BBC Radio, 22 September 2019.

3. Tom Wilson of Goldsmiths University.

4. *Neoliberalisation and 'Lad Cultures' in Higher Education*, Alison Phipps and Isobel Young, Sociology, 2015.

5. The Appendix to this chapter gives the full list of suggested reforms.

Chapter 9: Regulation and Pressure

1. *Today Programme*, Radio 4, 2 August 2019.

2. *File on 4*, BBC Radio, 3 October 2019.

3. BBC News, October 2016.

4. OfS was established in January 2018.

5. Office for Students Website. Mission statement.

6. Blog by Nicola Dandridge, OfS website, 23 October 2019.

7. Blog by Nicola Dandridge, OfS website, 23 October 2019.

8. Office for Students, website, 9 January 2020.

9. See Chapter 1.

10. *A review of evidence for bystander intervention to prevent sexual and domestic violence in universities*, Public Health England, 2016

11. *Changing the Culture: Tackling gender based violence, harassment and hate crime*, Universities UK, October 2019.

12. *Tackling racial harassment: universities challenged*: Report by EHRC, October 2019.

13. Professor Julia Buckingham, comment on Racial Harassment report by EHRC, UUK website, 23 October 2019.

14. Wellcome Foundation website, 27 June 2019.

15. Wellcome Foundation website, 27 June 2019.

16. Wellcome Foundation website, 27 June 2019.

17. Wellcome Foundation website, 27 June 2019.

18. GenPol website.

19. 1752 website.

20. *Recommendations for Disciplinary Processes into Staff Sexual Misconduct in UK Higher Education*, The 1752 Group and McAllister Olivarius, September 2018.

21. TUC website, announcement of formation of the Coalition, 26 June 2019.

Chapter 10: Starting Afresh

1. UCU website.

GLOSSARY

EHRC	Equality and Human Rights Commission
FRIES	Sexual consent should be: Freely given, Reversible, Informed, Enthusiastic and Specific
GuildHE	Guild of Higher Education
LSE	London School of Economics and Political Science
NUS	National Union of Students
OfS	Office for Students
UCL	University College, London University
UCU	University and College Union
UUK	Universities UK

INDEX

Absolute Research, 7, 11
Academic staff
　juniors staff, 51–53
　professors, 52
　teaching staff, 31, 57, 152–153
Advisory Conciliation and Arbitration Service (ACAS), 14, 108–109
Advocates, 44, 189, 208, 235–236
Ahmed, Sara-Director of Feminist Research at Goldsmiths University, 96
Alcohol
　and consent, 39–40
　drunkenness, 34
　effect of, 40
Alienation, 161
Ambassador programme, 178
American Health Care, 179
Angiolini, Elish, 44, 52–53
Anglia Ruskin University, 125–126
Appeal, right of, 122, 126, 205
Argentina, 155
Aristotle, 168
Arts Council of Great Britain, The, 138
Attenborough, David, 177
Australian Human Rights Commission, 18

Baird QC, Vera-Victims' Commissioner, 31, 61, 112, 126, 146–147, 223
Banter, 40, 74, 147
Barber, Michael-chair of OfS, 8
Bartoli, Marion, 168
BBC
　BBC News Reports, 26
　File on 4, 100, 223–224
　investigation, 32
Beer, Janet, 16, 67
Bennett, Alan, 38–39
Bill's New Frock, 188
Birmingham University, 102, 183
Bisexuality, 8
Bishop's Mill Pub, Durham, 33
Boar, The, 35–36
Bola, JJ, 166, 173–174
Boston Marathon, 168
Bristol University, 97
British Board of Film Classification, 166
British Heart Foundation, 234
Brook, 7
Brunel University, 61, 115–116
Buckingham, Julia, 16–17, 61, 190
Buckley-Irvine, Nona, 149
Bullingdon Club, The, 39
Burnell, Jocelyn Bell, 138
Bystander
　intervention, 184–185
　training, 182, 184–185, 230–231

Cambridge Analytica, 155
Cambridge University, 97, 100, 102–103, 105, 111, 178, 204
Campaigns
　coalition, 239
　hub of, 237
　local, 234–235, 240
　national, 6, 235
Canadian Parliament, 155
Cancer Research, 234
Cardiff University, 183
Central Lancashire University, 151
Chapman, Emma, 25, 99

Charities, 108–109, 138
Chief Executives of companies, 137
Children's Commissioner, The, 151
Clifford, Max, 108
Closed community, 144–145, 176, 207
Clubs
 officers of clubs, 209
 rugby clubs, 148, 185
 sports clubs, 58, 148, 209
Communications, 76–79
Complainants
 gender of, 235–236
 needs of, 127, 239
 rights of, 205
Complaints
 anonymous, 116
 record, 22–23
 sexual abuse, 8–9, 24
 sexual assault/rape, 66
 sexual harassment, 201
Confidence and self-esteem
Consent
 nature of, 208
 training, 44, 178–182
 workshops, 178, 179
Conservative Party, 39
Corbyn, Jeremy, 169
Corpus Christi College, Oxford, 1
Coventry University, 8
Culture Change. *See* Universities UK (UUK) publications

Daily Mail, 97
Dandridge, Nicola
 when Chief Executive of OfS, 228
 when Chief Executive of UUK, 13, 229
Darwin, Charles, 164
Data Protection Act, 78
Desert Island Discs, 49
Detachment
 detached tone of procedures, 196
 of senior managers, 196
Dignity, 14, 176, 243
Dignity Advisors, 115
Dobson, Andrew, 97
Donellan, Austen, 65–66

Drucker, Peter, 206–207
Dunn, Peter-Director of Press and Media, Warwick University, 27–28
Durham University, 5–7, 33, 35, 95, 97, 148, 167
Duty of care, 65, 112, 196
Dweck, Carol, 189–190

Edinburgh University, 178
Education Select Committee of House of Commons, 240
Empowered Campus, The, 146
End Violence against Women Coalition, 5, 224
Enforcement of policies and procedures, 224
Equality and Human Rights Commission (EHRC), 231–232
Equality and inequality
 in Britain, 137
 in universities, 137
Essex University, 99
Evening Standard, 99

Fat Girl Rodeo, 35
Feminism, 174
Fenton, Kevin, 29
Fenton, Rachel, 230–231
Fiction, role of, 188–189
Field, Mark, MP, 168
Field trips, 46–48
Finance Directors of companies, 137
Financial Times, 155
Fine, Anne, 188
Fraenkel, Eduard, 1
Freedom of expression, 84, 145
Freedom of Information request authors
 authors' letter to universities, 4
 nature of authors' request, 107–109
 results of authors' request, 20
 BBC, 101
 Guardian, 152–153
Friendship groups, 56, 214

FRIES, approach to issue of consent, 179
Funding of universities, 141

Galloway, Scott, 155
Gays, 15
Gender
  bias, 2
  discrimination, 170
  pay gap, 137–138, 138
  studies, 70
GenPol, 182, 235–236
Giugni, Lilia, 182
GMB trade union, 237
Goodlad Initiative, The, 185–186, 211
Government intervention
  2016 approach to UUK, 4, 13
  disadvantages of, 225
  selective approach to, 225
Government Minister for Universities, 26
Greenfield, Susan, 189
Greenpeace, 168
1752 Group
  foundation, 236
  Power in the Academy: staff sexual misconduct in UK Higher Education. (With NUS), 7–8
  Silencing Students: Institutional responses to staff sexual misconduct in UK Higher Education, 26
Guardian, 6, 38, 80, 96–97, 102, 103, 152–153, 171, 228
Guild of Higher Education (GuildHE), 200
Guilt, 54–55
Guinness, Dan, 185, 211

Hallien, Pierre, 186
Halls of residence, 128, 146
Hall, Stuart, 108
Harasser, pass the, 83
Harassment advisors, 205–206
Harman, Harriet, 45

Harris, Rolf, 108
Hart, Celia, 180–181
Heads of department, 154
Hidden Marks. See National Union of Students (NUS) publications
Hinds, Damian, 140
Historic cases, 118
Hite, Shere, 164
Hogg, Robert, 148
Homophobia, 149–150
House of Commons, 155, 240
Huffpost, 180–181
Human Resources Departments (HR)
  attitude of, 157–158
  criticism of, 88
  work of, 89
Hymas, Charles, 166

Independent Sexual Violence Advisor (ISVA), 182
Independent, The, 6, 96, 154, 156, 183, 194, 224, 239
Information gap, 15–18
Initiation tests, 36
Insecurity, 143–144, 158
Inverdale, John, 168
Ireland, 155
ITN, 137–138

Jackson, Clare, 101
Javid, Sajid, 3
Johnson, Boris, 39, 169
Johnson, Jo, 3
Judges, 78, 165

Katehatis, Alexandra, 151
Keble College, Oxford, 39
Keele University, 94, 97
  Sexual Violence and Support Team, 114
Kelly, George, 190
Kemp, Gene, 188
Kennedy, Helena, 183
King's College, London, 65–66
Kingston University, 60–61
Klute Nightclub, Durham, 33

Lad culture and laddism, 36, 147–150, 238
Lady Margaret Hall, Oxford, 1
Lamb Sir Norman, MP, 60
Lawlor, George, 182
Leadership, 4, 154, 240–241
League tables, 141, 194–195
Leicester University, 58, 100
  Leicester#MeTooOnCampus, 234–235
Lester, Julius, 170
LGBT, 150, 170
Liberal environment of universities, 57
Lodge, David, 1–2
London, 25, 87–88, 111, 235
Lorenz, Konrad, 164
Louisa, 32
Louise. See FRIES, approach to issue of consent
LSE, 148–149
Lucky Jim, 1–2

Manchester University, 176
ManMade, 137, 139, 168
Mansfield College, Oxford, 183
Mansion House, 168
Marketisation and commercialisation of universities, 142–144
Martin, Sally, 139
Masculinity and manhood
  male entitlement, 2
  male stereotypes, 190
  masculine identity, 40
  pressure on men, 87–88
Master's Degree, 10
Media, 5–6, 10–11, 27–28, 45, 93–106, 111–112, 156, 225
Mediation, 77, 123, 202
Melbourne University, 172–173
Members of Parliament (MPs), 137
#MeToo Movement, 59, 74, 156, 234
Millionplus, 200
Morris, Desmond, 164
Motivation, 192–193

National Union of Students (NUS) campaigns, 3
  publications
    Hidden Marks, 2010, 60, 238
    Power in the Academy: staff sexual misconduct in UK Higher Education (With 1752 group), 2018, 237–238
    Sexual Violence in Further Education, 2019, 238
    That's What She Said (with Alison Phipps), 2014
National Union of Students (NUS) publications, 3, 33, 64, 170
Neoliberalism, 142
Newcastle University, 183–184
New York University (NYU), 155
Non-Disclosure Agreements (NDAs)
  BBC revelations about NDAs, 26
  Emma Chapman and NDAs, 25
  Goldsmiths and NDAs, 96
Northumbria University, 60–61

Office for Students (OfS)
  equivalent in Wales, 229
  legal powers of, 228
  regulatory framework, 227–228
  welfare of students and, 227–229
Olivearius, Anne, 153
Oregon. See Harasser, pass the
Oriel College, Oxford, 132
Outsourcing, 142–143, 158
Oxford University, 1, 39, 180, 186–187

Page, Tiffany, 40, 44, 152
Parliament, 137, 240
Penis, 40, 149–150, 164–165
Perception, 90
Perpetrators (and alleged perpetrators), 32–37, 41, 80–84, 108, 112, 152, 156
PhD
  students, 49–51
  supervisors, 49
Phipps, Alison, 36, 142, 209

Pinsent Masons, Solicitors, 67
Plagiarism, 56–57
Plato, 86
Pleck and Sawyer, 165
Police
  attitude to university disciplinary action, 131–132, 153
  Metropolitan Police, 115–116
Policies
  dignity and respect, 200–201, 203, 207, 209
  equality and diversity, 176
  sexual harassment and abuse, 128–129, 134, 200
  welfare policies, 227
Pornography, 37–38, 150–152, 165–167
Postgraduates, 5, 8, 35, 94–95, 212
Power
  abuse of, 217
  imbalance of, 213–214
Predators, 1, 3, 41, 43, 106, 152–153, 216
Prevalence of sexual abuse, 11
Price, Hannah, 94
Private lives, 212, 214
Procedural justice, 112–113, 126
Procedures, 107–135
  anti-harassment and bullying, 203
  complexity, 120–121, 157–158
  dignity at work and study, 176
  disciplinary, 88, 119, 127, 232–233
  grievance, 119
  legalese, 120–121, 202
  not written for complainants, 205
  sexual harassment and abuse, 134
  student complaints, 77, 119, 127
  student conduct, 119
Professors, 41, 138, 140, 152
Public agencies, 230–232
Public Health England, 5, 230
Public relations (PR) and publicity, 207
Pull A Pig, 35
Purnell, Sonia, 169
Pye, Annie, 154

Queen Mary and Westfield College, 66
Queer, 8, 149–150

Racial harassment in higher education, 231
Ramakrishnan, Venki, 49
Rapunzel, 188
Regulations. *See* Procedures
Report and Support, 117, 120–121
Reporting sexual abuse
  anonymous reporting, 75, 105, 116–117
  under-reporting, 9–10, 22–23, 74–75, 105, 203, 236–237
  where to report, 4, 238
Reputational damage, 24, 26–27, 71–72
Reputation of universities, 20, 25, 29, 71–74
Research organisations, 232–234
Revolt Sexual Assault, 6–7, 9–11, 97
Risk assessment, 95
Roman Catholic Church, The, 6
Rugby, 147–149, 179, 185–186

Sanctions, 55, 177
Sarah Green, 5, 69, 224
Sathyamurthy, T.V., 45
Saville, Jimmy, 3, 108
Scandals reported in the media
  Birmingham University, 102
  Bristol University, 97
  Cambridge University, 97
  Durham University, 96
  Essex University, 99
  Exeter University, 94
  Goldsmiths, London University, 96
  increase in reports, 97
  Keele University, 94
  LSE, London University, 148–149
  mismanagement, 21
  Sussex University, 94–95
  Trinity Hall, Cambridge University, 101
  University College, London University, 106
  Warwick University, 98

S4 Capital, 155
Schools, 38, 186–188
Security staff
   role of, 146
   training of, 115–116
Segal, Lynne, 38–39, 162, 173
Semple, Jack, 168
Serial offenders, 101, 152
Sexual Harassment and abuse
   banter, 40, 74, 147
   flashing, 3, 34, 146
   flirting, 74
   groping, 1, 3, 5, 34, 146
   kissing, 3
   rape, 27, 32, 36, 64
   stalking, 3, 60
   touching, 1, 3, 5, 65
   verbal abuse, 65
   violent assault, 10, 88
Sexual harassment at work, 231
Single sex education, 38–39
Skidmore, Chris, MP, 26
SOAS, London, 178
Social media
   Facebook, 35–36, 155
   Rapechat
   Snapchat, 97, 234–235
   YouTube, 171
Sorrell, Martin, 155
Specialists, sexual abuse
   numbers appointed
   shortage of, 115
   training of, 115, 244
Sponsorship, 71, 85
Sports, 58, 148, 162, 178, 209
Srivastava, Kalpana, 170
Star performers, 84, 85
St Hugh's College, Oxford, 44, 52–53, 132
St John's College, Oxford, 205–206
Stone, Norman, 1
Student Room, The, 6–7
Student services, 24, 70, 95, 115
Sun, The, 7
Surveys
   Brook, 7, 9–10
   local, 11, 12
   need for authoritative, 193–195
   NUS/1752, 9–10
   Revolt Sexual Assault, 6–7
   Sun newspaper, 7
   Youthsight (The Telegraph), 5, 11
Sussex Men's Rugby, 179
Sussex University, 5, 94–95, 142, 179
Swain, John, 187–188
Swetman, Joshua, 168
Switzer, Kathrine, 168

Tab, The, 182
Taskforce of UUK, 4–6
Taulke-Johnson, Richard, 150
Telegraph, The, 4–5, 36, 93, 166
Tenure, security of, 143
#ThisIsNotWorking Alliance, 238
Thunberg, Greta, 177
Times, The, 58, 96
Trades Union Congress (TUC), 238, 240
Trinity Hall, Cambridge, 101
Trump, Donald, 154–155
Turbulent Term of Tyke Tiler, The, 188–189

UCL, University College, London, 97, 99, 180
Unison, 237
United Church, 169
United Nations (UN), 175
Unite the Union, 237
Universities Australia, 17–18
Universities UK (UUK)
   attitude to commissioning a survey, 19
   budget, 19
   chief executive, 13, 229
   nature of, 224
   president, 16
   publications, 3, 16, 67, 194, 224
      Changing the culture: Report of the Universities UK Taskforce examining violence against women, harassment and hate crime affecting university students, 2016, 4

Tackling gender-based violence, harassment and hate crime: two years on, 2019, 228, 235–236
Tackling online harassment and promoting online welfare, 2019, 16–17
staff of, 194–195, 228, 235–236
University and College Union (UCU), 6, 32–33, 152, 237–238, 244
University College, London, 25
University of Bath, 21
US President, 15

Valois, Ninette de, 139
Verkaik, Robert, 39
Vice Chancellors, 12–13, 19, 65, 109, 183, 193, 199, 243
Victim/survivors, 31, 34, 41, 52, 79, 89–90, 105, 117–119, 199, 227
Victoria Derbyshire Show, 182
Virgo, Graham, 98

Wagener, Karli, 58, 100
Wales
 minister for education, 229
 Welsh Government, 226–227, 229

Warwick University, 27, 35–36, 80, 98, 181–182, 205
Weinstein, Harvey, 3, 156
Wellcome foundation, 232–234
Westmarland inquiries, 96–97
Westmarland, Nicole
Whitely, Leila, 40
Wilkin, Lesley, 154
Willis, Paul, 149
Wilson, Elizabeth, 164
Wimbledon Singles Title, 168
Women's Football Club (Sussex), 179
Women's Liberation Movement, The, 2
Woolf, Leonard, 38–39
WPP. *See* Sorrell, Martin

York University, 183
Youthsight, 5

Zellick
 chair, 66
 principles, 67
 revision of, 68–69
 taskforce, 66–68
Zero Tolerance, 4, 22, 83–84, 88, 118
Zuckerberg, Mark, 155

www.ingramcontent.com/pod-product-compliance
Lightning Source LLC
Chambersburg PA
CBHW051605230426
43668CB00013B/1984